FOUL!

THE SECRET WORLD OF FIFA: BRIBES, VOTE RIGGING AND TICKET SCANDALS

ANDREW JENNINGS

HarperSport

An Imprint of HarperCollins*Publishers*

First published in hardback in 2006 by
HarperSport
an imprint of HarperCollins
London

First published in paperback in 2007
This abridged edition is produced exclusively
for FourFourTwo in 2011

1

A CIP catalogue record for this book is
available from the British Library

ISBN 978-0-00-789599-1

Printed and bound in Great Britain by
Clays Ltd, St Ives plc

The HarperCollins website address is
www.harpercollins.co.uk

For more on FIFA, see the author's website at
www.transparencyinsport.org

This book is proudly printed on paper which contains wood
from well-managed forests, certified in accordance with
the rules of the Forest Stewardship Council.
For more information about FSC,
please visit www.fsc.org

Mixed Sources
Product group from well-managed
forests and other controlled sources
www.fsc.org Cert no. SW-COC-001806
© 1996 Forest Stewardship Council

For the bears and for the fans

ANDREW JENNINGS is an internationally acclaimed investigative journalist and film-maker. His exposé of sleaze at the International Olympic Committee, *The Lords of the Rings*, is ranked among *Sports Illustrated's* Top 100 Sports Books of All Time. It was translated into 13 languages and earned him a five-day jail sentence from a judge in the IOC's home town of Lausanne.

Foul! has so far been translated into 12 languages and Jennings' BBC *Panorama* documentary *The Beautiful Bung*, based on the book, has been screened worldwide. See more at www.transparencyinsport.org.

CONTENTS

ABOUT THE AUTHOR

When children ask me what it is I do exactly, I tell them I've made a life and a living out of chasing bad men.

I've investigated corrupt police-officers, corrupt governments and professional criminals, I've won awards for my work on secret British involvement in the Iran/Contra scandal and crooked cops. And when I turned forty I started looking into sport.

Sport? Some of my comrades in investigative journalism asked me, had I gone soft?

Not a bit of it. Sport belongs to the people. It's part of our culture, the social cement that holds us together.

And just as corruption in government and among police officers causes public concern, so, too, it matters when bad men take control of the people's sport and use it for their own personal ends.

So I trawled the waters of sport politics and came up with one gigantic fish, rotting, as fish tend to, from the head. It was, of all things, the Olympics.

I revealed that Juan Antonio Samaranch, leader of the Olympics, had been a career fascist, a minister in the government of the murderous Spanish dictator Franco. And I discovered that among the men who stood behind him in his International Olympic Committee were some who should have been behind

bars (and have since spent time there) and many for whom
Olympic politics was not a way to serve the people, but self-
service, big time – and supersize that.

Investigative reporters don't always live to see bad men get
their comeuppance, but the whole world saw Olympic corruption
blow up back in 1998 and when the US Senate investigated the
scandal they invited me to testify in Washington.

I might have left it there. But then I got a call from Colin
Gibson, sports editor of the *Daily Mail*, asking would I take a
look at the people running international football. 'Ah, come off it,
Colin,' I said. 'Football is *big*. It would take years to find out
what's going on inside FIFA.'

It's taken years. The things I've discovered have shocked even
me. Some bad guys have been in there taking what they can. It's
still the beautiful game, of course. They can't take that away from
us. But, as you'll read here, there's been some ugly business going
on. I'd like to see the beautiful game get the leadership it deserves.
In that spirit I dedicate this book to the fans.

PREFACE

Click, click, click
Candid snapshots from inside world football's fortress
But stop
That's not allowed in the villa up on Sunny Hill

They say it's the people's game
Don't ask, how much the boss pays himself
Or who got the kickback, who got the contract
Don't ask, who got all those World Cup tickets

They're based in Switzerland
Where whistle-blowing is a crime
Their documents are forever hidden
Nobody ever gets the evidence

This isn't a history of FIFA
Just a taste of the truth
Here are snapshots of how it really is
How it's been for the last quarter century
For the good of the game.

Andrew Jennings
February 2006

BLATTER'S TICKING TIME-BOMB

A kickback lands on Sepp's desk

FIFA Headquarters, Zurich, winter 1998. It's just turned seven o'clock in the morning at Sunny Hill, the white-walled, red-tiled mansion perched on a hillside high above the city at Sonnenberg. Down in the warm basement mailroom, secretaries gather to collect the post and telexes and overnight faxes. News of football results, player transfers, tournaments, travel schedules, pleas for subsidies from national associations, appointments with heads of state – just an ordinary day's business at the world's largest sports organisation.

Heads of department pop in, eager to pick up some tit-bit of news they can take upstairs and present, personally, to the boss, in exchange for some small favourable comment, or just a nod of approval. Here comes Erwin Schmid, FIFA's Director of Finance, a broad-shouldered bear of a man, who gets more dishevelled as the day goes on, his shirt-tail escaping from his trousers. Here comes Erwin, with the usual happy greetings.

He picks up an envelope. It's from the head office of FIFA's bankers, the Union Bank of Switzerland. Erwin tears it open and looks at the enclosed document, a notification of a payment. His plump face pales. He reads it again. Something is not right. Something is most irregular. Erwin leaves the mailroom and heads for the elevator, gripping the document in one tight, nervous hand.

Two floors up, FIFA General Secretary Joseph S Blatter, known universally as 'Sepp', reclines behind his leather-topped desk, in a high-backed black leather chair, performing his morning ritual of reading the *Neue Zurcher Zeitung*. The big JVC television is silent, too early for the tennis he loves to watch.

At 61 years of age Blatter has the air of a man who's in charge. He's a round man, round face, round body, a little on the short side, going bald. But his well-cut suit, his two-tone shirt, his solid gold cufflinks, his heavy, premium wristwatch, his don't-waste-my-time stare, all say: *I've been the boss for 17 years. Now, what can you do for me?* President Joao Havelange has an office just above but today he's an ocean away, at home in Brazil. Sepp is in charge.

Blatter enjoys the villa's finest views. A gigantic picture window frames the distant Alps, the wooded ridge and, far below, the lake and the old city, its church steeples squeezed between the valley shoulders. He might stroll across to the side window and gaze down on a steep vineyard and secluded villas whose high gates open now and then as a trickle of dark Mercedes saloons carry their owners to the city.

But this is no day to enjoy the view. His finance director has bad news for the boss who is also his good friend, indeed, his best friend. Erwin Schmid tells colleagues, 'I have only one friend in my life and that is JSB.' And now Erwin has the kind of news that can tear friendships apart. As the elevator rises, Erwin's spirits sink.

For the past three years Blatter himself has overseen the sale of rights for the World Cups of 2002 and 2006: the rights to show the games on television in every country in the world, the rights to put FIFA's badge and the magic words 'World Cup' on soft drinks, beer, burgers, razors and trainers. They're all in FIFA's gift. And senior people within FIFA have overseen a whopping US$2.3 billion worth of business to old friends in a secretive company a few Alpine ranges to the south.

Sitting at No 10 Marktstrasse in the little tax-haven city of Sarnen, this company goes by the name of International Sport and Leisure, or ISL.

Erwin steps out of the lift. The document in his hand threatens to blow FIFA apart. Over the years there's been unkind talk of the relationship between FIFA and ISL, rumours of kickbacks and bribes. Loyal fellows like Erwin have dismissed that talk. Special relationships always attract gossip, don't they? Bad losers often complain. And there's been no evidence of wrongdoing. But now, there's this piece of paper. A payment has landed some-where it shouldn't.

Erwin pads along the carpeted corridor. He reaches Blatter's door, knocks and waits for the call. In he goes. Erwin wastes no time. He hands the document to Blatter. It is a standard USB form, stating that ISL has transferred one million Swiss francs (some £400,000) into FIFA's account. It's the payee's name that makes acid churn in the belly. He's a senior official in football. It's a very fat 'thank you'. This is most improper (but not illegal in Switzerland, as long as it is declared to the taxman).

'My God,' Blatter groans. He stands up. 'This is a problem . . .'

'*It does not belong to us.*'

Erwin knows that. But what will Blatter do? Call in the police? Report it to FIFA's Executive Committee, to the Finance Committee? That is the least that should be done.

Instead, the money is moved out of FIFA's account to the man named on the payment order. And the record of the transaction sits there. The law says this record must be kept until the winter of 2008. So there it is, a ticking timebomb, waiting to go off.

Tick. Tick. Tick.

Tunis, Abou Nawas Hotel, 23 January 2004. The reporters have come from Cairo and Cape Town, Yaounde and Nairobi, some wearing city suits, some in white desert jalabiyyas, others in colourful West African agbadas, all sitting in rows, notebooks at the ready, waiting for the words of the most powerful man in world football.

High above the podium in the brightly lit function room is the portrait that dominates public buildings, restaurants and shops in this country. President Zine El Abidine Ben Ali stands erect and unsmiling, sports a helmet of implausibly jet-black hair and wears a long dress-coat, studded with medals. In the Tunisia he has led since 1987 no serious political opposition is permitted, no critical opinion tolerated, and hundreds of people rot in jail after unfair trials. There are elections here: Ben Ali wins them every time, claiming 99 per cent of the vote.

But his country always shows a happy face to tourists and, this week, to thousands of fans from Rwanda and Benin, Mali, Zimbabwe and a dozen other countries who've flocked to the stadiums on the Mediterranean coast for non-stop, stadium-shaking drumming, cheering and jeering at the finals of the 2004 African Nations Cup.

Here comes Sepp Blatter, taking his seat at the centre of the podium beneath Ben Ali's portrait. He was general secretary, now he's FIFA president with six years under his belt. Blatter admires

Ben Ali as someone who has earned 'a lot of respect' and praises Tunisia as 'an absolutely open country'.

To Blatter's right sits our host, Issa Hayatou from Cameroon, president of African football for the past sixteen years. A big, broad-chested man, once a champion 800-metre runner, Hayatou looks tired but has a nod here and a smile there for men he's laughed and duelled with. Eighteen months ago he challenged Blatter for the FIFA presidency. He promised to 'restore integrity and accountability' to the organisation. Along with others, he wrote to Zurich's public prosecutor accusing Blatter of corruption and demanding an investigation. Hayatou's integrity campaign couldn't beat Sepp's charisma and Blatter won a second term as president. The prosecutor decided not to take Blatter to court, on the basis that there was insufficient evidence for a prosecution to proceed. No charges were brought.

Everyone knew Blatter would strike back. It's his way: *stand in my path and it will cost you.* Yesterday, Hayatou stood for re-election as president of the African confederation. Blatter and his Zurich bag-carriers strongly backed the challenger, Botswana's Ismail Bhamjee. But Hayatou is no pushover. He'd secured his base in the French-speaking countries from Morocco down through West Africa to the Congo, and Bhamjee, who never got any momentum, lost, 46 votes to 6. Still, Blatter's a pro. There's no trace of bitterness in his face. He touches Hayatou's arm and the gesture says, *We're all friends again.* The subtext: *I'll get you next time.*

To Blatter's left sits FIFA General Secretary Urs Linsi who, like his president, sports a diagonally striped tie, blue shirt and dark suit. Like Blatter, from the German-speaking part of Switzerland. Like Blatter, he's balding; one rogue tuft of hair sticks up above his forehead.

Ever since arriving at FIFA, Linsi has been a Blatter-man.

Blatter recruited him as finance director from Credit Suisse years ago in 1999. When then-General Secretary Michel Zen-Ruffinen backed Hayatou for the presidency, Linsi stayed loyal. After the votes were counted in Seoul in May 2002, Blatter growled to a Swiss reporter, 'Tomorrow, we take care of Mr Clean.' Mr Clean, Zen-Ruffinen, was out. Linsi was on his way up. So now, aged 54, Linsi's got two jobs, finance director and general secretary. He's a very powerful man.

At the Abou Nawas Hotel, a question from the floor. What does the president think of African football? Blatter smiles. He says with conviction, 'Africa is the future of football.' (It's a formula that works for him. About the women's game? That firm voice: 'The future of football.' About Asia? 'The future of football.') Blatter's on good form, flashing his warmest charismatic smile. It's a beautiful day.

But there's a party pooper. Me. I've got hold of the roaming microphone. 'A question to President Blatter.' His smile fades, he draws up a fist to support his chin. I'm not his favourite reporter. I know about the ticking time-bomb. And here I go: 'After the last marketing and TV contract was signed with ISL for 2002 and 2006, a secret payment of one million Swiss francs from ISL arrived by accident in FIFA's bank account.'

I draw breath. Sepp's eyes tighten a little. I'm off again. 'It is alleged that you, as general secretary at the time, instructed it was to be moved immediately to a private account of a FIFA official.' Then I ask him who it went to.

Blatter tenses up, gazes down at the table before him and mutters something about the ISL company, now in the hands of a liquidator. Then, he says, frostily, 'I will not enter into discussion here in this press conference and I think also it is totally out of the matter we like to discuss today in Africa together with the African journalists for the development of football in this continent. I'm sorry, please accept this situation as it is and I am sure your colleagues from the African and international press here will agree with me.'

Outside, in an atrium dotted with tall potted palms, I sink into a soft leather settee, sip strong sweet coffee and chat with old acquaintances from the press-room at the previous World Cup. A tall white reporter from South Africa, hurrying to an interview, pauses, waves and calls cheerily, 'I always like to see some theatre!' A lean magazine editor from the Gulf, casual in open-neck shirt and unbuttoned sports coat marvels, 'Blatter's face went green!'

'No,' says a friend from the Kenyan *Daily Nation*, 'He turned yellow.'

Tick. Tick. Tick.

2

GOODBYE SIR STAN

Hello to a New World of Sport

Frankfurt, 10 June 1974. Voters descending through the clouds could see the River Main snaking under bridges and around the toy-town skyscrapers in the distant city. The modest glass tower of their hotel poked up from the pine forest close to the airport. There in his suite their president, Sir Stanley Rous, watched the planes coming in, from other European cities or faraway continents, heard the squealing rubber and bumps of their touch-downs.

Rous was a tall, upright schoolmasterly man with an authoritative grey moustache, a man pushing eighty, reserved as only an Englishman of his generation could be. Would this plane carry men steadfast in their loyalty? Or waverers? Or men open to inducements? Or enemies who wanted him to take his pension and go? Wanted to sweep him away, change everything and bring in a new and totally different way of life?

Sir Stanley leaves the window and returns to the round wooden table that dominates his sitting room. Not long now. Tonight: a big party thrown by the playboy Gunter Sachs, he'd been married to Brigitte Bardot. Tomorrow: the congress and the election, the threat from the Brazilian Joao Havelange ('Jow' he calls himself). Surely Sir Stanley's steady hand, cautiously reforming the laws of the precious game and his determination to protect it from the spivs who wanted their logos plastered everywhere, would prevail against the challenger?

Football was in good heart, Sir Stanley believed. Since becoming FIFA president thirteen years ago in 1961, he'd steered the sporting ship well clear of murky political waters. There was no need to rush to recognise Communist China and he'd been absolutely correct to ban Arsenal from going to play there. He wasn't going to banish Taiwan. And if the natives in places like Sharpeville mobbed the police, tragedies were bound to occur. He'd done his reading and he knew that fellow Mandela was a Red and football would take no benefit from siding with convicts. His mission, as he saw it, was to bring people together, not exclude old friends from the game. And the law was the law. If the elected South African government passed laws saying that blacks and whites shouldn't live together, FIFA had no right to interfere. It was dismaying that here in Frankfurt this week were so many people who couldn't understand that his sensible point of view was in the best interests of the game.

His men at the English FA had distributed his election programme, there really wasn't much more to do. The World Cup was starting in a few days and keeping his eye on that ball was an obligation he wouldn't shirk. Meticulous organisation was essential. That's why he'd received a knighthood, for putting together the joyous Olympic Games in London back in 1948. The Queen had even made him a Commander of the British Empire.

All this fuss about elections and for what? FIFA hadn't needed one before. Rous had taken over from Arthur Drewry, which made for 18 years of English rule at FIFA, a marvellous stretch. Why change things now? But some of the London newspaper reporters had reservations. Was that disloyalty? They were calling him bluff, outspoken, immovable – although that last point wasn't fair, he'd listen to anyone. They harped on about his age but 79 was a good age, he'd got at least four more years in him. He was football's ambassador to the world. There would be more than 120 men from football associations here in Frankfurt for the election and surely enough of them would not be troubled – or even aware – that his campaign was being described in London as 'ponderously inept'. Those chaps had done well to raise the money for their fares. And what was this colossal piece of cheek? Joao Havelange, the challenger, offering him a generous pension!

There's a knock at the door. 'Mr Myers from the United Press International to see you, Sir,' and in bustles Morley Myers, polite, on the short side, in his dark striped suit, crinkly hair and glasses, always scurrying to file another dispatch. Morley comes bearing news Sir Stanley doesn't want to hear, news that no-one else dares tell him.

'Your rival is running very strongly, he's everywhere, there doesn't seem to be much aggression or lobbying on your side.' Morley wants Rous's response: 'How do you feel about this? What's your political platform?'

'I let my record speak for itself,' Rous replies.

JOAO HAVELANGE never missed a chance to speak for himself. For four years he'd tugged sleeves, made his promises, struck his deals. With voting just hours away he couldn't afford to waste time in his suite. Every hour planes landed bearing voters

– new ears to whisper into. The Airport Steigenberger was a modern airy building but pressman Myers, talking to me thirty years on, recalls, 'There were lots of hidey holes and they were all meeting surreptitiously, little plots going on all over the place, and you didn't know who was who. That's where the real election was taking place. You have this antennae and somehow you could sense that FIFA was about to experience this seismic change, an end of a way of life. There was a buzz, you could feel it.'

Sir Stanley's rival was a knight as well, but even more so; three different governments had bestowed the honour on him. He was a Portuguese Knight of Sport, a Knight of the Infant Enrique, and a Swedish Knight of Vasa and, although this wasn't written down anywhere, a darling of the generals who then governed his homeland, Brazil. Havelange was promising to bring some diversion, some prestige to their discredited regime and the generals would help him in any way they could.

Havelange looked presidential, the aristocratic nose a domineering prow cleaving his way through wavelets of lesser beings, the hooded dark eyes penetrating to the depths of their wallets. The tall athletic physique, the gleaming brow, the swept back hair, the rakish curls, the finely-cut clothes, all made for an imposing impression. He looked hungry, a predator with curling lips that hinted at sexual power.

Rous was a great referee, he could run all day and was a man you'd trust with your watch and keys, but he wasn't a work of art. Screaming girl fans didn't lie in wait to tear souvenir strips from his black tunic and shorts. Havelange had swum in the 1936 Olympics and was back again playing water polo in 1952 in Helsinki. He had poise. He had grace and ambition beyond medals. When he climbed the ladder out of the pool for the last time he kept going upwards. Four years later in Melbourne he

11

was Brazil's Chef de Mission, two years on and he'd taken control of the Brazilian Sports Confederation – including football – and in 1963 he joined the select ranks of the International Olympic Committee (IOC). There he learned to network on a global scale and so impressed his colleagues that half a lifetime later, in 1999, the IOC appointed him to their anti-corruption commission.

Havelange at 59 was two decades younger than Sir Stanley, and vibrating with energy and ideas. Unlike the ageing president who only spoke English, Havelange could tell you fluently in any one of four languages how much better off you'd be if you voted for him. He talked of his successful business career. He ran Brazil's biggest bus company, had interests in chemicals and insurance. He promised that with his entrepreneurial dynamism there'd be money galore to create wonderful new competitions and training courses.

Many of the officials flying in to stay at the Steigenberger had met Havelange and liked him. He'd brought Brazil's World Cup winning team to play in a country near them, thoughtfully leaving the gate-money behind with his grateful hosts.

He'd listened to their troubles. Across Africa people were angry that it was so hard to qualify for the World Cup. There were 16 slots for finalists and nine were reserved for Europe. South America had bagged four and that left only three for the rest of the world.

Havelange would set that right. Within eight years, he pledged, there'd be 24 finalists and he dropped strong hints that the extra eight places would go to teams from the developing world. Rous's FIFA, dominated by Europeans for all its 70 years, wouldn't listen to Africa. It was if they couldn't hear non-European voices. At their UEFA congress in Edinburgh earlier in the year they'd made a threat: *increase the number of finalists and Europe withdraws. We'll take our ball away and run a European World Cup and invite a 'few South Americans'.* Sir Stanley, deaf to the sound of voters running towards Havelange, couldn't see a problem with a European World Cup.

Havelange told the press that he'd win, said he had more than 70 votes pledged. 'It won't be on the first ballot,' he said. 'Besides, there are always surprises in elections and, like everyone else, I have to wait.'

THE MAN both Havelange and Rous were waiting for, hoping he would win the election for them, had driven from his offices two hours away in France, checked in to the airport hotel, changed into a plum-coloured suit and mingled with the voters. What neither of the contenders then knew was that both had called for help from this shy but determined man who, backed by his team of fixers, was becoming the most powerful figure in world sport. Morley Myers recalls, 'Horst Dassler was the invisible man, blending into the background, very wealthy but not ostentatious and it was a case of seeing the guy but not knowing what he was doing. We didn't realise then how involved he was.'

Dassler's day job was running his family's Adidas sportswear company. He wanted sports federations to sign contracts that committed their teams to wear Adidas kit. He wanted individual stars to wear the three stripes. And he wanted the world to watch on television and follow their example. To get the contracts, he had to have the sports leaders in debt to him. What better way than to put them in power?

He surveyed the likely candidates, did his private deals, and helped them to victory with Adidas money. He made them presidents and let them remember – charmingly of course – that he could keep them in power, or push them out. All they had to do was play the game, which meant looking out for Adidas. And now power at FIFA was up for grabs. It was a sport shockingly under-sold to the public and Dassler had plans to address that. But first, the elections.

When it came to Rous versus Havelange, Dassler's strategy was to back both horses, at least at first. 'I had to be as close as possible to Havelange,' says Christian Jannette, a small, dark, intense linguist, then a member of Dassler's discreet Adidas international relations team. Jannette had joined Dassler after working for the French team at the Munich Olympics two years before. 'I knew Havelange from my relationships with the IOC,' he said.

Sir Stanley was looked after by the third member of Dassler's platoon at the Steigenberger, John Boulter, the British former 800-metre runner. Boulter, a tall, lean, languages teacher with floppy blonde hair tumbling over his beaky nose, seemed taken aback at being asked what he actually did in the great FIFA war of succession. 'I can't remember a lot from 30 years ago,' he told me. 'I was just nice to Rous. One just helps and is friendly, and why should one not be? Whatever Christian Jannette says, I don't have any specific recollection of being nice to Sir Stanley. I certainly wouldn't be nasty to him. It's a long time ago.'

Jannette's memory is sharper. 'Boulter had to be as close as possible to Stanley Rous – Dassler did not take any risks! Dassler at 38 was very sporty and fit and every morning he jogged with Boulter. This was something new for me. I was always very far behind!' A woman sports official told me once that the first time she met Dassler she was more than impressed, she was mes-merised. It wasn't that he was tall and very well built, it certainly wasn't the sizeable nose. 'It was the eyes,' she said, 'They held you suspended in the air.' Dassler could inspire great devotion and Boulter, a hard veteran of 30 years of sports politics, elections and kit contracts, told me that he wasn't up to writing a biography of Dassler 'because it would be a hagiography'.

Jannette, the unwilling jogger, fondly recalls a charismatic and complex character. 'Power and business were important to Horst. I don't think money was important. He could have had a Rolls-Royce with a driver, but he had none of that. Once we were invited to a big party in Germany and he had no evening dress – he had to rent one. He did not have a lot of taste, nor care about these things. Power in the world of sport meant he could have his people anywhere.' Was he a nice man? 'Not always. He could be very, very charming but he could be very, very bad. Terrible.'

A fourth member of Dassler's team checked in, again with a specific mission. Colonel Hassine Hamouda, a Tunisian athlete who had competed for France in Berlin in 1936 when Havelange swam for Brazil, published a sports magazine for the Franco-phone countries. It was called *Champion D'Afrique* and it was funded by Dassler. Adidas would never sell a lot of kit in Africa but Dassler gave it away to win the support of officials whose votes could be decisive in elections. Hamouda helped focus attention on his generous boss and his wishes. Morley Myers explains how it worked. 'Rous was unhappy about commercialising the game, that wasn't his world, and he didn't realise the influence of Horst Dassler and Havelange. Horst at the time had good contacts in Africa. He gave away a lot of equipment so that was support the African countries couldn't do without. It seemed pretty obvious that if Havelange didn't get in, you wouldn't be getting any more gear.'

Sir Stanley couldn't speak directly to the voters from the Francophone countries but Havelange could. French was his first language, the one he spoke at home with his parents who had arrived in Brazil as immigrants from Belgium. Not only did Havelange speak their language, he understood French anxieties. France had hosted the founding of FIFA in Paris in 1904, Frenchman Jules Rimet had got his name on the World Cup, but power was slipping away. 'It was clear that France was not supporting Rous. Havelange was their candidate,' says Jannette. 'In that time France was losing power. At the IOC Lord Killanin had defeated Count Jean de Beaumont to be president. There was a big fight between the French and English speakers. French had been the first language at the IOC and English second. Now it was reversed.'

American journalist and fluent French-speaker Keith Botsford, who was in Frankfurt for the London *Sunday Times*, says it wasn't just the French football association backing Havelange. French diplomats had put in a word for Joao in the old French empire. 'I saw a lot of African diplomats in Frankfurt, some of them the cream of the French education system. Some were absolutely not of football, not necessarily voting but influencing their delegations,' said Botsford.

Dassler kept a cautious foot in both camps until the fifth member of his election team turned up and took him to the bar. 'Rous isn't going to win, he's lost a lot of Africa,' he said. He knew because he'd been at the African confederation congress and Havelange had his people there. 'He [Havelange] is catching up fast and I think he may win. You have to talk to him now.'

Dassler then simply distributed a wad of cash among the officials who were holding out or who could bring in other votes to encourage them to back Havelange. There is no evidence that Havelange knew what Dassler was up to. Each was given a few thousand dollars and those who were not in their rooms found an envelope when they got back.

So Dassler was now backing one horse and it was Havelange. Jannette turned up the charm. 'I was there to be as friendly as possible with Havelange and to go to the official reception. I didn't even go to the Congress.' He laughed. 'And I nearly missed the World Cup Final. That day in Munich I had a very nice lunch with Monique Berlioux, Director of the IOC, and Leni Riefenstahl, and we spoke and we spoke and suddenly I noticed I had to be in the stadium and I arrived at the beginning of the second half. Adidas had good seats in the VIP stand and Dassler was not pleased with me.'

AFTER AN EARLY breakfast on the morning of Tuesday 11 June 1974, the voters from 122 national football associations, their hangers-on, the fixers and reporters queued for coaches that took them the 10 km into the city and off-loaded them outside Frankfurt's Kongresshalle, grand in the old style, on the banks of the broad grey Main. They filled only the front few rows of the auditorium.

In their hands they had Havelange's eight-point election programme. Damn the Europeans, the size of the World Cup would be expanded and he would introduce a Junior World Championship. He would go out and find sponsors and with their money he would give cash aid to national associations, courses run by visiting coaches, doctors and referees, new stadiums and more competitions in the developing world for developing clubs. The headquarters in Zurich would be expanded.

If Rous had opened FIFA's door to China that morning he might have split Africa and carried with him the powerful Secretary-General of the Supreme Council for Sport in Africa, Jean-Claude Ganga from the Congo. That might have been enough to secure four more years in power. Instead the usually avuncular Ganga was provoked into striding the gangways of the auditorium haranguing delegates as they came forward to cast their votes. Havelange predicted correctly. It did go to a second ballot. He needed 79 votes for a clear victory on the first round but got only 62 to Sir Stanley's 56. The second round gave

Havelange world football, 68–52, before it was time for lunch.

A few days later Keith Botsford told *Sunday Times* readers what had happened in the Steigenberger and the Kongresshalle. He reported, 'a pungent odour of money and the too-familiar strains of *Rule Britannia* once again sinking beneath the waves'. And he wrote of 'little brown envelopes being passed around with such fraternal sentiments as "if that's not enough, please tell me"'. Things could only get worse, he feared. 'Sir Stanley was a bulwark protecting football against the twin evils of Too Much Money and Too Much Politics. Havelange is a creature of the Too Much.'

The Steigenberger emptied and the lucky ones went on to the World Cup. 'The day after I went to fix up an appointment to see Rous again,' says Morley Myers. 'And they said, you can see him now. Normally he used to be surrounded by his allies and I went up and he was there by himself sitting at this huge round table and he was stunned. He was traumatised.

'"I'm shocked, I treated Havelange as my son and he stabbed me in the back," he said.

'I said, "No, it's politics, winners and losers." He was a very forlorn and lonely figure. My story was headlined: "LONELY KNIGHT AT THE ROUND TABLE". It was like seeing a beaten champion. I don't think Rous expected any of this, he was going on past record and he didn't expect the French, the Greeks, the Africans to turn against him and there were some people he thought were his friends and they weren't.'

Sir Stanley was given the consolation title of honorary president and lived another dozen years, making it to Mexico for the 1986 World Cup and dying two weeks after Argentina defeated Germany 3–2. By then the world of football he had led was under the control of the spivs he'd fought to keep at bay.

SEPP BLATTER, MADE BY ADIDAS

A new leader rolls off Dassler's production line

IF HAVELANGE couldn't deliver on his extravagant election promises and come up with a bigger World Cup and eight more teams in the finals he would be a one-term president, a football failure, a dead man in four years time when he met his voters in Buenos Aires on the eve of the 1978 World Cup. He needed money, lots of money, and he relied on Horst Dassler to get it for him.

For Dassler, this was going to be bigger business than selling sports kit. Football didn't know yet but it was about to be shaped into a commodity. Dassler sent John Boulter to London to run an eye over fresh-faced super-salesman Patrick Nally who was making a name for himself persuading companies to sponsor sports and pay for coaching in return for good publicity.

Dassler invited Nally to his headquarters at Landersheim in Alsace, just inside France. Forget little England, he said, throw in your lot with me and work the whole planet. Together they created a company in Monte Carlo to sell the marketing rights they'd bought from sports federations – including football rights from FIFA. The silver-tongued Nally and the charismatic Dassler pulled off a coup enticing one of the world's biggest brands, Coca-Cola, to invest heavily in Havelange's development schemes. They'd help fund coaching, new tournaments, refereeing courses, all sorts of good things. In return Coke got to plaster its logo all over the World Cup.

Once Coca-Cola had signed up, everyone wanted a piece of the action. Sponsors competed for the right to use FIFA's badge and slap the words 'World Cup' on their products. They got lots of free seats for entertaining business contacts and rewarding loyal staff. They also got to mingle with football officials and athletes. 'I told Pele over dinner last night that he always made his best moves when played a square ball,' is one-upmanship that *can* be bought.

The news of Horst Dassler's great achievement in the corridors of the airport hotel was greeted thoughtfully in the committee rooms of world sport. The era of volunteers giving up holidays, weekends and evenings to run international organisations was waning. If the brilliant Dassler could pension off the patrician Sir Stanley, what else might he achieve?

'Money like you've never known it,' he replied over long lunches. Once, he just wanted the athletes wearing the three stripes and trefoil of Adidas. Now he wanted the whole sport. A new word entered the vocabulary of sport: 'support'. Dassler deployed his team to 'support' favoured candidates. And when they'd won they returned the favour, selling him the right to market their logos, their entire sports, their athletes' achievements, to commercial sponsors. The new federation leaders got money to develop their sports with more events, more trainers and more facilities.

They were praised in industry handouts, soon reflected in the press, as wise leaders who had brilliantly brought new money into their sports.

The language of sport was rewritten and the word 'sponsors' moved aside to make room for the more friendly 'partners'. Nally spent half his life in the air wooing new partners from Japan to New York. Sugared drinks and fatty burgers were promoted by well-rewarded athletes whose own diets were carefully balanced for fitness and health. The administrators, even the ones who ran second in their elections, were comforted with first-class air travel, five-star hotels, generous expenses, honoraria and pensions all paid for by the big corporations. Dassler breathed new life – and money – into the General Assembly of International Sports Federations, a talking shop for sports leaders. And he gave them a home, a plush villa in swanky Monte Carlo.

Dassler, a man unknown to the fans, was becoming the puppet-master, controlling the leaders of world sport. Ambitious officials begged him to marshal his team behind them, organise their campaigns, bring in the votes. He was a generation ahead of his competitors. A highlight at every congress and committee meeting of most Olympic sports was the Adidas dinner in the hotel banqueting suite, fixers making nice to the officials. As elections drew near in the world's best-loved sports the big question was: 'Who's Dassler supporting?' Once in place, and so long as they behaved themselves, these winners had Dassler's protection. Only extreme old age or death could separate them from power. Eventually, presidential elections weren't held for decades at a time at track and field, the IOC and FIFA.

The fixer team grew with full-time employees and part-time agents positioned throughout the international federations. Some had responsibility for continents or ethnic and language groups, others looked after their boss's interest in specific sports. Dassler hired the petit German fencer, Thomas Bach, who rose to become a leading member of the IOC. Dassler sought out the big, blustering Anwar Chowdhry from Karachi, who scoured the East forcing athletes into Adidas strip, and with Dassler's 'support', took control of world amateur boxing in Bangkok in 1986. Olympic boxing swiftly degenerated into fight-fixing and bribery but Chowdhry survived because, as he once boasted to me, while guzzling breakfast yoghurt in his Houston hotel bedroom, 'I know many things.'

Dassler's agents worked to fix which cities got to stage the Olympics. At the heart of his network was the IOC president's top advisor, the silver-haired Yugoslav Arthur Takac. From his office in Lausanne he oiled Dassler's relationships with IOC members and his burly son Goran channelled bribes from cities keen to be hosts. Goran went into business with Russian IOC senior statesman Vitaly Smirnov.

In 2004 BBC television's *Panorama* reporters posed as businessmen keen to bring the Olympics to London in 2012. They met Goran Takac and, on camera, he explained how it was done. *Pay me the money and I'll get you the votes*. That was the end of his Olympic career.

Always the visionary, Dassler had anticipated that it was best to have journalists on your side. He sponsored the Munich-based fortnightly newsletter *Sport Intern*. Publisher Karl-Heinz Huba helpfully set the media's agenda, filling his pages with 'exclusive inside information' that freed some reporters from the bother of working to find their own stories. Huba boosted Dassler's companies. Dassler's critics, business rivals and the remaining few faint voices in sport who didn't want Coke's money were traduced. Long after Dassler's death *Sport Intern* remains alive and kicking. The sheet was a great supporter of millionaire Korean

IOC member (and secret intelligence agent) Kim Un-Yong who went to jail in 2004 for fraud.

NINETEEN SEVENTY-FOUR was the watershed year. As Havelange flew back to Rio with FIFA in his pocket, the top sports official in the dying Franco dictatorship in Spain reached out to Dassler. The sharp-faced and diminutive Juan Antonio Samaranch had met Christian Jannette at the Munich Olympics. 'Samaranch was chief of protocol of the IOC and I had to work a lot with him and we became very good friends,' Jannette told me. 'In 1974 Samaranch knew that I was working with Horst and he told me that he would be interested to meet him. He invited us to Barcelona to his home and we spent two or three days there. He was Chief of Protocol of the IOC and people often say that the chief of protocol is the next president. I knew that Samaranch would like to be president.'

That year Samaranch was a vice-president of the IOC and on 18 July in Barcelona was at the forefront of the annual parade of ageing fascist comrades, celebrating their civil war victory in 1939 and giving the right-arm salute. It was the last time he'd do this in public. His mentor and patron, the dictator General Francisco Franco, died the following year.

Samaranch made the pilgrimage to Landersheim, Dassler's HQ, played tennis with Horst, the pact was agreed and 'support' was put in place.

Next in line for the Dassler treatment was track and field. Dassler supplied athletics kit all over the world. Now he wanted the television and marketing rights to the sport. He looked around for his kind of man and found Primo Nebiolo, from Turin, malleable, greedy and eager to get on. They liked each other, and Dassler gave Primo Adidas support.

Sometimes the valuable marketing rights of the sports federations, their championships and their badges took a roundabout path on their way to the jazz 'em up departments of Coke, McDonald's and the other 'partners'. Having waved bye-bye to their owners in Zurich, Lausanne or London these contracts swirled around the Swiss Alps for a few weeks, touched down briefly in some lawyers' offices and then came to rest in the centre of the country in the beautiful little town of Sarnen, population 9,000, by the lake and under the mountains. For a while Dassler parked FIFA's multi-million dollar marketing rights with an obscure company called Rofa, owned by Bayern Munich manager Robert Schwan and the club's greatest star Franz Beckenbauer. Beckenbauer moved on to other Swiss-based business activities and the sports rights crossed the road to live with another Dassler company, also based in Sarnen.

With business booming Dassler needed money to expand. One man who had it was André Guelfi.

'I REMEMBER going from Monte Carlo on the back of this boat which was zapping along at a zillion, million miles an hour towards St Tropez where André Guelfi lived,' remembered Patrick Nally, the English super-salesman. 'I suppose there were some questions about where his money came from, but having a big yacht and big cars was very helpful for Horst because he could entertain people in style.'

Lean and muscular André Guelfi lived at high speed on land and water, and piloted his own jet planes He was one of the most stylish hustlers of the twentieth century, now in his nineties yet still sharp-eyed and quick-brained, doing business deals as fast as ever. Decades before he met Dassler the young Guelfi made his first fortune hauling sardines out of the Atlantic, raced Grand Prix cars and competed at Le Mans in 1953. Guelfi socialised with the royal family in Morocco and then, unwisely, with their thuggish opponents. He made friends with gangster actor Jean-Paul Belmondo and bought property in Paris. It was whispered that Guelfi was a bearer of grudges and if you crossed him you should forever glance over your shoulder. He was, after all, buddies with the chief of France's secret intelligence service.

In the late 1970s Guelfi acquired half of the sportswear company Le Coq Sportif and sponsored Tour de France winner Bernard Hinault and tennis player Arthur Ashe. Dassler, wanting to broaden his base away from the Adidas brand, bought the other half of Le Coq and found in Guelfi a kindred spirit with money to invest. Together they bought from the Russian communists and sold to the capitalists the marketing rights for the 1980 Olympics in Moscow. Guelfi had acquired great wealth from somewhere he wasn't talking about but a chunk of it came in handy when they had to cough up 45 million Swiss francs for the marketing rights to the 1986 World Cup in Mexico.

Dassler set up a new company to specialise in selling the rights. He called it International Sport and Leisure, forever to be known as ISL.

Energetic support from Dassler and Guelfi levered Juan Antonio Samaranch into the presidency of the IOC in 1980. He responded warmly, giving Dassler the Olympic Order, gold version, and the marketing contracts for more than a decade of Olympics. The following year Dassler and his team arranged the installation of Italy's Primo Nebiolo at track and field without the uncertainty of an election. Primo went on to rig medal results at world championships, bought steroids wholesale for Italian athletes and sold his sport's marketing rights to ISL. The new IOC president moved to live in Lausanne and so did Guelfi, choosing a lakeside villa with sublime views across the pure waters of Lac Leman to the casino dome in Evian. Guelfi enjoyed it and Samaranch coveted it, and for a mere US$4.4 million of IOC money it became the construction site for Samaranch's monument to himself, the Olympic Museum.

As Samaranch expanded his Olympic empire, recruiting the new post-Soviet nations of Central Asia, he flew by private jet, owned and piloted by Guelfi. They dropped in several times on Uzbekistan and later travelled to do business in Beijing. 'We were masters of the universe,' Guelfi told a reporter.

Dassler had built a bright, gleaming influence-building machine. Into one end went cash, favours and men with more ambition than scruple. Out of the other came sports leaders branded with the Adidas trefoil. Over time, in the marble and gilt lobbies of the upmarket hotels where sports business was now done, people asked: were these men really the leaders of their sports, representing the interests of athletes and fans? Or were they agents of influence, puppet presidents, owing their primary loyalty to Dassler?

But Dassler still hadn't got full control of the mansion up on Sunny Hill, looking down on Zurich. Blocking Dassler's way was FIFA's general secretary, the long-serving Helmut Käser with his fuddy-duddy insistence on respecting protocol and convention. In 1980 Dassler began a dirty tricks operation to drive him out. Anonymous letters stuffed with disgusting allegations and rumours of kickbacks circulated. This 'Kill Käser' campaign was put on hold when a report commissioned by the conspirators from a private detective was sent accidentally to Käser.

Käser demanded an explanation from Dassler who also said sorry. Six months later Dassler was spreading word that the general secretary's days in office were numbered. This time Käser confronted the hard-eyed Havelange who, concealing a blade in his sleeve, insisted his job was safe. It was, for several weeks. Then, in late 1980, Havelange dispatched a four-page letter to Käser with a list of instructions. If he failed to obey any one of them, he was out of the door.

JOSEPH 'SEPP' BLATTER had joined FIFA in 1975 to manage their new Coca-Cola funded schemes to produce more coaches, referees and specialist sports doctors. He'd made the headlines four years earlier when he accepted the presidency of the World Society of Friends of Suspenders, a group of 120 men from 16 countries, who 'regret women replacing suspender belts with pantyhose'.

The big money deal with Coca-Cola was signed in May 1976 and in the formal photo a miserable looking Käser sits next to a hooded-eyed Havelange and one of Coke's promotions men. Standing behind and leaning over Käser is Blatter, a youthful looking man in an immaculate cream double-breasted sportscoat with fashionable wide lapels, dark shirt and a kipper tie with a large geometrical pattern that appears to be living a vigorous life of its own. The trousers are trendily flared, as every man about-town's were in the mid-1970s, and although the hairline is already retreating, the long lock draped carefully across his brow gives him a dashing air. He leans forward and looks up from beneath his eyebrows with a sly, confident smile that says, *You know you want me, Baby . . . is that a suspender belt you're wearing?*

Blatter had trained in business administration but his skills were in public relations. In 1964 he got his dream job in his favourite sport, general secretary of the Swiss ice hockey federation. Forever after, Blatter kept a souvenir hockey stick in pride of place in his office. Dassler, looking to recruit a director of development, spotted Blatter eight years later, working for the watch and race timing company Longines. Aged 39 the handsome Blatter with the warm, open smile was hired. General Secretary Helmut Käser was not consulted about the appointment and barely saw his employee for the first six months. 'Blatter was trained at the Adidas headquarters at Landersheim before he went off to FIFA,' recalls Patrick Nally. 'He spent his time there working alongside Horst, getting to know the Adidas operation. Horst and Blatter became very close during the months he lived in Landersheim. He was very much cemented into the relationship.'

'HORST DASSLER absolutely wanted to get rid of Helmut Käser,' recalled André Guelfi in 2004. 'So Horst said to me, "Couldn't you organise something to get rid of him? Dispense with him, but not physically?" I told Horst, "I'll deal with it."' Guelfi is still upset at suggestions that he would stoop to violence. 'Contrary to what you have heard I am not a killer,' he says. 'I succeeded in convincing Käser to hand in his resignation, I said to him, "If you don't, your life will be made a misery, and everything will be hard. They will try to make you make a mistake, to find faults, to put you in a difficult position, to sack you."'

Guelfi told Käser that he had no future in the new FIFA. 'You know when a boss wants to sack someone, he can do it. So, my advice was we try to negotiate a smart exit and reap a golden handshake. Sick at heart he agreed to resign. I don't remember anymore how much he got but it was a lot of money.'

Money wasn't the only reason Helmut Käser thought it wise to get out. Something sinister was lurking in the Zurich shadows. According to Guelfi, 'Käser said to me, "I am being followed." I said to him "I don't know if you are being followed. But, if they are having you followed it is to try to make you stumble. They will try to get you one way or another so what's the point, you are better off leaving with your dignity intact and negotiate your safety. Because the bottom line is, what's important in life, at your age, you are not going to look for another job", and I persuaded him just like that and I negotiated, although against Dassler's wishes, that he got the maximum figure.' Guelfi paused and added, 'If he was really being followed, it was Horst Dassler.'

Guelfi had done the deed. Pliant Harry Cavan was happy to complete the paperwork. Cavan was a FIFA vice-president for nearly 30 years, an Ulsterman representing the four home British associations on the FIFA executive committee. If anybody could have stood up to Havelange it was Cavan with the moral weight of the founders of the world game. But Cavan was too busy counting the money he got from Dassler as a 'shoe consultant'. Brian Glanville, doyen of British soccer commentators, says Cavan 'grovelled' to Havelange. Former Northern Ireland captain Derek Dougan noted that Cavan, once a lowly-paid trade unionist, 'did very well out of the game and had a tremendous lifestyle'.

On 3 September 1981 Cavan wrote to one of FIFA's Swiss lawyers enclosing two cheques to get rid of Käser, total value 1,597,000 Swiss francs. 'Should you wish to have any more information,' said Cavan, 'please contact Mr J S Blatter.' The IOC gave Cavan an Olympic Order. Havelange, without consulting his executive committee, announced the name of Käser's replacement. And off the production line rolled Adidas's latest product: Sepp Blatter, FIFA general secretary.

Says Guelfi, 'Thanks to Dassler, Monsieur Blatter was appointed, just like that. Dassler said to me, "We are going to put this fellow there, he's alright, he is one of us." I can tell you, Blatter was Dassler's lackey. I found Blatter really insignificant, especially next to Havelange. He was, for me, like a floor sweeper. Blatter can say whatever he likes, making you believe he has done it all on his own. The truth is he owes his job to Dassler. Blatter was really in awe of Dassler, anyone could see that, you did not need a degree to see it, how he spoke to Dassler, how he was with him. We often used to meet for lunch at Landersheim and it was as if Blatter was in the presence of God.'

In the late 1990s French magistrate Madame Eva Joly was investigating corruption at the state-owned Elf oil company. She called Guelfi in to interrogate him about allegations that he had laundered US$40 million to bribe politicians in France, Europe and Africa.

He said he couldn't remember anything so she had him locked up for five weeks. By now he was close to his 80th birthday and the experience refreshed his memory. Guelfi reportedly talked about money laundering through Olympic bank accounts, claimed to have spent US$138,000 on air tickets for Jacques Chirac (before he became President of the Republic) and that whatever he did, he was 'working for France'. That prompted IOC vice-president Vitaly Smirnov to intervene, writing to Ms Joly on his IOC-headed notepaper demanding his old friend's release. While locked up in La Sante jail Guelfi was a few cell doors away from Bernard Tapie, the owner of Marseille football club, jailed for fraud and tax evasion, who had bought the Adidas company from the Dassler family. In 2003 a Paris court fined Guelfi US$1.2 million, gave him a suspended three-year jail sentence and, aged 84 and incorrigible, he set off for Moscow to discuss investing in the national rail system. A Paris appeal court later increased his fine by US$750,000 and said he must serve 18 months jail time.

Käser's widow recalled later that despite the shabby way Havelange treated him the only time she ever found her husband weeping was two years after his dismissal. He came home distraught. He'd met a friend in the street who had been a guest at the marriage of the Käser's daughter Barbara. She'd neglected to tell her parents of the event. Who was the groom? Sepp Blatter.

Horst Dassler died of cancer in 1987, aged 51, and his businesses were inherited by his son, his daughter and four sisters. The sports officials he had promoted did their best to airbrush him out of their history. Dassler, once the most powerful and influential man in sport, who had made them rich, was an embarrassment. He didn't make it posthumously to their halls of fame because his name would always remind them of their shame. The Adidas company has changed hands – and the probity of its practices – twice since Dassler's death.

Havelange would never forget that his general secretary was Dassler's choice, 'one of us' appointed to serve the interests of his companies. Neither would Sepp Blatter, the official whose values came branded with the three stripes of Adidas.

SEPP MAKES HIS MOVE ON HAVELANGE

... and lives to tell the tale

Estadio Monumental, Buenos Aires, 25 June 1978. Joao Havelange's friends, the gold-braided and decorated Generals and Admirals seated around him in the VIP box, were ecstatic. The electrifying Mario Kempes had scored twice, then set up the third in extra-time. Argentina had beaten the Dutch 3–1 to seize the World Cup in front of a crowd that at last had something to cheer about at home. It was the FIFA president's first championship since pensioning off Sir Stanley Rous and a triumph for him and the Argentinian military dictatorship. Under the menacing glare of the soldiers surrounding the pitch, patrolling the gangways and staking out the approaches to the stadium, Havelange smiled and said, 'The world has seen the true face of Argentina.'

Certainly it was the face that Argentina's brutal government wanted the world to see. The World Cup did for them what the

1936 Olympics had done for Adolf Hitler. Another murderous regime had exploited sport and sportsmen and basked in their reflected glory.

The true face of Argentina, was, perhaps, the brave and fearful face of the women, the mothers of the disappeared, who risked arrest and worse to parade around the capital's Plaza de Mayo every day of the World Cup, bearing pictures of their missing loved ones, victims of the junta's dirty war against their own people.

Human rights demonstrations around the world had failed to have the 1978 tournament moved to another country, any country as long as it changed governments through the ballot box. When the generals seized power two years earlier FIFA's only concern was, would this interfere with staging the event? Perhaps Havelange felt personally concerned; one of his companies in Brazil had reportedly insured the championship.

The world's newspapers reported that the generals, determined to eliminate any opposition, had ordered their critics tortured in military barracks and then disposed of. For many this meant having weights strapped to them, being bundled into air force planes and dropped, screaming behind their gags, limbs flailing, tumbling down, down to where the estuary of the River Plate met the deeper waters of the Atlantic. Havelange brushed aside these reports. What had this to do with FIFA?

They'd had 25 days of glorious football, and now that Argentina had won convincingly there'd be no more dark whisperings about how they'd managed to knock in an astonishing six goals, two more than needed to make the final, past a suddenly lacklustre team from Peru who had in the first round held Holland to a goalless draw. Why shouldn't Argentine President General Videla visit the Peruvian dressing room before the game? The Argentine junta's sudden offer to the Peruvian junta of huge grain shipments and US$50 million in loans couldn't affect what happened on the pitch, could it? Bundles of cash for the team? Just sour gossip.

And well done Admiral Lacoste, Carlos Alberto to his friend Havelange. Once he'd taken over from General Omar Actis, the money had really flowed. Actis, with his talk of tight budgets and staging the World Cup on the cheap, had been the wrong man to put in charge of the organising committee. Those allegations that dear friend Carlos Alberto had been behind the gunning down of Actis in a Buenos Aires street? Just idle talk.

President Havelange was indeed a good friend to the Admiral and cheered when he became President of Argentina, if only for 11 days, in December 1981. The following year Admiral Lacoste became a vice-president of FIFA and held the position for four years. When democracy returned and Lacoste was investigated for the surge in his wealth and the purchase of a splendid residence in the coastal resort of Punta del Este in Uruguay during the years of terror, Havelange stepped in to save his skin, and helpfully explained that he had personally lent Lacoste US$90,000.

FOR HAVELANGE, life at the top was a succession of four-yearly acclamations by the FIFA congress. Lucky to assume power in the 1970s as business got seriously interested in buying sport, he and Dassler and later ISL kept their promises and Sepp Blatter efficiently put together the FIFA coaching courses and the new youth tournaments. The Europeans, cowed by the Brazilian's icy stare and the money he was laying out around the poorer countries, didn't dare run a candidate against him at the congress at the Spanish World Cup in 1982, or in Mexico in 1986 or even in Italy in 1990. And as soon as that championship was over Havelange told a South American reporter that he would offer himself for further acclamation, for a sixth term, at the next FIFA congress in Chicago in June 1994.

So why was general secretary Sepp Blatter sidling around the corridors of the congress of African football in Tunis in January 1994, under the unsmiling portraits of President Zine El Abidine Ben Ali, whispering in delegates' ears that the old man had had a fine run, done a marvellous job for the game but now, at 78 for goodness sake, surely it was time to go? After thirteen years in the shadows Sepp had had enough. He couldn't bear to wait any longer. Churning in the guts, Sepp lusted to be President.

Havelange promised one thing and did another. 'I would like to retire,' he said one day, 'and I can see Blatter as my successor . . . we can build him up.' Sepp was about to prepare his campaign for a seamless transition when he heard the familiar voice again: 'I spend 300 days a year travelling. I sacrifice myself for the youth.' And it seemed Havelange was happy to continue sacrificing himself.

Perhaps it's true what they said in the kitchen at Sunny Hill, that the old fellow really was being injected with live cells from baby cows in his quest for eternal life, and at the same time, milking a wonderful lifestyle out of FIFA. Things looked hopeful for Blatter for a while after Havelange had a dizzy spell in Barcelona in 1992, but he rested and was soon back on the road again.

But then he went too far. They were in Las Vegas in December 1993 for the World Cup final draw, Coca-Cola produced a souvenir bottle, Daryll Hall sang the tournament anthem, and Caesars Palace had announced that Pelé, the only soccer player the Americans had heard of, was to be the star of the draw for next year's first round groups. At last FIFA was launching soccer bigtime in the world's biggest market – and then Havelange snatched the guest list and drew a line through Pelé's name. And just because Pelé had publicly attacked the Brazilian Football

Confederation, the CBF, which had been run by Havelange's son-in-law Ricardo Teixeira for the past three years.

Banning Pelé spurred *Playboy* magazine in Brazil to look into the unexplored territory of Havelange's background. They dug into his past business dealings. They also examined his father's role in the arms trade. With the generals long out of power, *Playboy* felt safe to investigate the topsy-turvey finances of the Brazilian sports confederation in 1974 when Havelange was in charge.

So Blatter was smiling and pirouetting in front of the Africans in Tunis, showing off his many talents. His aides from Zurich had their instructions: *spread the word, I'll make a great president.* Then he flew home to Zurich, put the lightweight suit in the closet, got out the thick overcoat and flew off to salty Nordwijk on the sand dunes south of Amsterdam. European soccer's top brass were gathering for their executive meeting. They had long memories, they'd never forgiven Havelange for defeating their man Rous in 1974 and they'd hoped a good European candidate would emerge. Well, here was Sepp Blatter.

'If you want to get rid of Havelange, I will stand against him,' Blatter told them. 'If you support me we can get rid of him.' It didn't go quite how he'd hoped. Ellert Schramm from Iceland came out of the meeting and told reporters, 'Blatter has proposed himself as a candidate for the presidency. He said, if you all support me, I will be the candidate. Everyone was astonished by his frankness. He was rejected. I said that we should discuss the disloyal General Secretary, not the President.'

Blatter tried to put his best gloss on it. He told reporters he had discussed the question of his candidacy with UEFA and if they believed he was 'the right man for football' . . . but then the idea had drifted into the sand.

Still hopeful, Blatter jumped into his Merc and sped off to the airport, bound for JFK. The general secretary always attended the congresses of the continental confederations and next on the schedule in the spring of 1994 was the Plaza Hotel, New York City. There would be 35 countries from the Caribbean and Central America and the Americans and Canadians, CONCA-CAF. When they voted together they could swing an election. Blatter was all set to campaign. Havelange also attended the New York congress and his burning eyes could have bored holes in Blatter's back. Havelange let it be known that he was still in charge.

'THERE IS something I have been wanting to tell you for some time,' said the President, having sent the minute-taker out of the Zurich boardroom. Havelange was alone with the presidents of his six confederations and a subdued general secretary. 'I have decided that when we go to France in four years time, there will be 32 teams in the final round.' It was what Africa and Asia and the Caribbean longed to hear. More slots for the developing world, more money from more television and more marketing. As they congratulated him on the eight more places he added, 'Did you really want to hang me because of Pelé?'

It was April and still two months to the congress in Chicago and the 1994 tournament. Blatter's ambitions were squashed. Would he survive the old man's wrath? People were already whispering about a shortlist of candidates for his job. Would he ever work again? Who would employ a man famous for trying to unseat his boss?

Perhaps it was Sepp's secretary who saved him. The Zurich officials, the general secretary's team in their smart uniforms, met in Los Angeles as the World Cup began and tall, short-haired Helen Petermann in the thick glasses nominated herself as shop steward. 'If he touches my boss we're all going on strike here, in America, with the media watching,' she declared. Havelange got the message and turned his attention to pampering the 200 guests he had invited from Brazil.

But it could only be a matter of time. The old man waited, maybe enjoying the daily fear in his disloyal general secretary's eyes. Blatter would be a meal eaten cold.

Meanwhile, Havelange exercised his president's prerogative and purged his committees. Especially pleasing was eliminating the Germans Gerhard Aigner and Horst R Schmidt who hailed from UEFA. They hadn't wanted Blatter but they had wanted the president out and now they would pay. Havelange made one special promotion, elevating his son-in-law Ricardo Teixeira to vice-chairman of the referees committee and putting him on the committee organising the next World Cup, in France.

Blatter wandered the corridors of Sunny Hill like a zombie. After Brazil beat Italy in Los Angeles he'd flown back, gone straight to his office and waited for bad news. It was six months coming. On the wintry morning of 10 January, while Blatter skulked behind his big black leather-topped desk, Erwin Schmid, acting on Havelange's orders, sacked FIFA's press officer Guido Tognoni and the director of competitions, Chilean Miguel Galan. Havelange announced he had lost confidence in them. Blatter's tale was that he had never sought to dethrone his leader and it was all a typical piece of nonsense dreamed up by journalists.

HAVELANGE WANTS TO GET SERIOUSLY RICH

Can he turn FIFA into a bookie's shop?

JOAO HAVELANGE ruled the wealthiest sport in the world but after twenty years in the job, it still hadn't made him seriously rich. Monarchs and dictators flattered as they led him to the best seats in their national stadiums, tycoons signed telephone number deals with him and *they* made millions – and how much was he making? When was *he* going to join the lists of the super-rich?

By the early 1990s Havelange had been a member of the IOC for 30 years, president of FIFA for nearly two decades and whatever he had made, it wasn't enough. How could sport make him as rich as he wanted to be? He looked around; where was the Big Idea?

If Havelange were to extract really, really big money from the game he'd need help. Tall, angular Jean-Marie Weber had been personal assistant to Horst Dassler and emerged as the top operator and public face of ISL after his death. It was said he worshipped Horst and photographs of the great innovator decorated the walls of Jean-Marie's office overlooking Lake Lucerne. Weber had helped map the shadier corners of the football business. Weber knew how to make Havelange rich.

Some of the ace salesmen in the expanding world of sports marketing were dismissive. 'Jean-Marie's not creative,' they'd say. They mocked when his bony face was looking the other way because he didn't come up with bundled 'packages' or new events that would need sponsors and could be sold to television. But that wasn't Jean-Marie's purpose. He had to get the business in. And he did.

Colleagues noted that wherever he travelled he carried two bulky briefcases. 'The confidential agreements,' they guessed. 'Jean-Marie would never trust his documents to a safe.'

A polite man, a lover of opera and fine wine, Jean-Marie knew how to cultivate people. He 'made nice' in every crowded hotel lobby and congress hall, shook every passing hand, kissed proffered cheeks and wrapped his long arms around the shoulders of old friends. When Jean-Marie sped across a room he was a skinny, pale grey-suited long-legged stork. You couldn't miss his mane of bouffant white hair and thin-rimmed glasses bobbing above the heads in a crowd or striding up the aisle at a stadium.

Let them laugh. He controlled the rights to three of the world's greatest sports tournaments: the Olympic Games, the World Athletics Championships and the Football World Cup. For a few days a year nearly every television screen in the world showed his programmes. But he still queued at barriers, clutching his ticket, to travel on scheduled air flights. He hadn't hit the big time yet.

Like Joao, Jean-Marie was looking for the Big Idea.

*　　　*　　　*

ERCILIO MALBURG thought he had it. The Brazilian business-man went first to Helio Viana, the backroom guy who managed Pelé's business affairs. Ercilio had the biggest of big ideas. If we can bend FIFA our way, we could run the most stupendously huge betting operation off the back of the World Cup, from qualifying rounds to the Final. We'll register the business in the Caribbean and clean up. Billions of dollars would flow in every year.

'You're crazy,' said Viana, 'you'll never make it acceptable to the laws in so many different countries. They'll regulate you out of business.' Pelé was not getting involved. There's the door.

Pelé had another, personal, business manager, Celso Grellet. Ercilio Malburg went to see him. 'I've got the connections,' he said. 'I know Canedo in Mexico, he's the longest serving member of FIFA's executive committee. He's a bigshot at Televisa, he understands how to make money out of football. And here in Brazil we have his close friend Havelange. What more do we need?' Grellet showed some interest but he couldn't see how to make the project work in so many jurisdictions.

But there was a Brazilian who loved to gamble and he snapped at the idea.

Matias Machline's parents came from Russia and made their new home in the southernmost cattle town of Bagé on the pampas near the Uruguay border. In 1961, at the age of 28, Machline set up the Brazilian arm of the giant Japanese electrical goods manufacturer Sharp. He made connections with the generals who seized power in 1964 and business flourished. When mili-tary rule collapsed in 1985 his good friend José Sarney, who'd fronted for the generals, became the first civilian president in two decades.

By 1990 Machline's family-controlled company was turning over a billion dollars a year and Matias Machline was one of

Brazil's leading racehorse owners – and gamblers. When the economy turned down in the early 1990s and business slumped, he cast around for another Big Idea.

His friend Antonio Carlos Coelho had set up the Banco Vega and it was thriving. Coelho and Machline were also friends of Johnny Figueiredo whose father was the last of the military presidents. Johnny loved the new sport of 'Futevolei'– a cross between beach football and volleyball. That led the old friends to start talking with Ricardo Teixeira about Ercilio Malburg's plan to make a fortune out of FIFA.

'We had one daughter, Lucia,' said proud President Havelange, 'and she has blessed us with three grandchildren, Ricardo, Joana and Roberto.' Their father was Ricardo Teixeira and the connection worked well for him. In 1989, although the marriage had crumbled, Joao installed Ricardo as president of the Brazilian Football Confederation, the CBF. Ricardo was also excited by Malburg's gambling plan.

Joao, Jean-Marie, Matias and Antonio came together at a four-star Miami North Beach hotel in mid-July 1993 – Ricardo couldn't make it. Richard Herson, an American vice-president of the Matias Machline Group, wrote in a top-secret memo to Sepp Blatter in May 2001, 'After months of informal discussions, this project was officially initiated on 27 July at a meeting in a suite at the Sheraton Bal Harbor Hotel.' Herson explained that Machline trusted him with 'the early co-ordination of this project as his direct executive assistant'.

Herson defined the project as 'the organisation of a worldwide, FIFA-endorsed membership club and lottery system dubbed FIFA Club which would operate a worldwide soccer lottery linked to FIFA sponsored events under a FIFA trademark licence.'

'A memorandum of understanding was drafted and signed by all present, except for Mr Havelange, who preferred that his name be unrecorded. All negotiations were therefore officially conducted with Mr Jean-Marie Weber.'

Within months Herson was counting his chickens. 'In a nutshell the conservative scenario projected pre-tax revenues of US$8.75 billion after year three, which would make it one of the largest gambling/lottery operations in the world.'

This was it. The Big Idea sought for so long by Joao and Jean-Marie. *Eight billion dollars a year and rising.* Think how big the little percentages would be, the commissions, the bonuses, the consultancies. Even the expenses would be grand.

Herson told Blatter, 'I recorded all materials pertaining to the project as well as discussions in several megabytes of aide-memoirs, designed to keep regular track of the project's progress, as well as links and participation of the various individuals and entities involved.'

The American had surprising revelations about what Jean-Marie was doing in the name of FIFA. 'With ISL's knowledge and agreement during the first half of 1994 these plans were presented and discussed with a number of organisations such as Caesars World and VISA International, in an effort to drum up interest and support for the project. Extensive negotiations among the original parties mentioned above were conducted in Dallas, London and in Zurich, usually at the centrally-located hotel where Mr Havelange kept residence.'

They hammered out a franchise that ISL would give exclusively to The Machline Group. Matias would be allowed to exploit the FIFA logo and its marketing rights for 'the development and exploration of selected activities'.

WORLD CUP '94 came to America and on 16 June in Chicago Havelange was given another four years power by acclamation.

The next day Germany opened the tournament against Bolivia. A couple of weeks later the businessmen were in session again at a 'conclusive working meeting' at the luxurious Mansion on Turtle Creek Hotel, in Dallas. A final contract was drafted and signed by Weber, Coelho, Machline and Herson. The same day, 3 July, Sweden defeated Saudi Arabia 3–1 in Dallas.

They met again at the Mansion on Turtle Creek 'for an additional preparatory session' on 17 July. The World Cup Final kicked off at lunchtime 1,400 miles away in Pasadena, California, where Brazil beat Italy 3–2 on penalties, but business was business. There were unbelievable amounts of money to be made. Matias Machline staged a welcome home for the winners and at a special event organised with Ricardo Teixeira they donated a television to each player and contributed several thousand dollars to a big thank you present.

A month later the businessmen from Europe and Latin America converged on a hotel in New York. They were joined by a new colleague, a business high-flier who'd quit the top slot at American Express Brazil to become CEO of 'FIFA Club'. It was 12 August and everybody signed the final contract. 'Operations were to commence soon after. It was expected that a number of large worldwide gambling and banking organisations would join the project soon afterwards,' says Herson.

Matias Machline, now aged 61, and his 30-year-old wife Maria Araújo said goodbye to their new gambling partners and drove off to Manhattan's East 34th Street heliport. At 8.30 pm the couple boarded a chartered helicopter bound for Atlantic City where Matias planned to play the tables.

Pilot Doug Roesch had passed all his tests for flying in normal visibility. But he wasn't experienced at coping with what pilots call inadvertent meteorological conditions – suddenly flying blind in cloud and relying only on instruments. After about 15 minutes in the air Doug Roesch contacted his home base. He said he was concerned about the weather conditions. He expressed hesitation about completing the charter.

Then Doug Roesch made radio contact with his colleague Eric Mansell who was piloting a sight-seeing flight over New York. Roesch said he was going to turn back – then he changed his mind and decided he'd make one more attempt to get to Atlantic City airport. Five minutes passed and they spoke again and Mansell said later, 'Roesch had changed from being worried and stressed to being relaxed and confident.' But it was very dark and he climbed to 2,000 feet trying to avoid the low cloud rolling into his flightpath.

Ten minutes later Mansell called up Rocsch to see how he was doing. The tape recorder in Mansell's cockpit recorded the brief exchange:

Roesch: Eric, I'm going inadvertent (*Distressed Voice*)
Mansell: Doug, are you kidding?
Roesch: Eric, I'm going inverted. (*Panicked Voice*)
Mansell: Doug, are you kidding? Are you kidding? Are you all right?
Roesch: Eric! (*Panicked Voice*)

A witness standing outside her home in a wooded area near Whiting, New Jersey, heard the helicopter overhead. She told investigators, 'All of a sudden, the motor noise changed to a slower sputtering sound. As I was trying to follow the noise, I saw a large orange glow begin to fill the sky.'

The wreckage impacted the ground vertically, making a crater fourteen feet in diameter and six feet deep. The skids were impaled in the ground. The subsequent inquiry attributed the accident to Doug Roesch's 'spatial disorientation'.

A FORMER PRESIDENT, leading politicians, a clutch of tycoons and his four sons and daughter attended Matias Machline's funeral. The Machline Group faltered without him at the helm and the family took the helicopter company to court claiming around a billion dollars compensation. The settlement is confidential but one source close to the case said, 'The family say that had he not been killed in this accident he would have made a giant, giant fortune on the FIFA lottery.'

Meanwhile Antonio Coelho had had another of his big ideas. He invested heavily in processing alcohol to fuel cars, lost a fortune and tried to bail out the business with money from his Banco Vega. Brazil's central bank stepped in on 15 May 1997 slapping a liquidation order on Vega.

A subsequent investigation by Brazil's Senate into corruption in Brazilian football contained six pages on the dealings between Banco Vega, the Brazilian Football Confederation and Ricardo Teixeira. Lucky Ricardo got nearly double the interest rate obtained by his federation and he just happened to withdraw all his money eight days before the bank collapsed. Despite his problems Antonio Coelho was thought by Ricardo to have such business acumen that he was appointed to the federation's finance committee.

A few days after the fatal helicopter crash Richard Herson was told he had late-stage lymphoma. Less than a month later, at the request of the heirs of Matias Machline, he travelled back to Brazil. In his memo Herson told Blatter the story of what happened. 'I met with Antonio Carlos Coelho and Ricardo Teixeira at a suite in the Holiday Inn Crowne Plaza in Sao Paulo, Brazil.

It was a very difficult and acerbic meeting, in which Mr Teixeira made it clear in no uncertain terms that he and Mr Coelho intended to pursue Mr Machline's Project, regardless of any previous agreements, to the detriment of Mr Machline's rightful heirs.'

He went on, 'At the time, in spite of our indignation, there was nothing we could do to counteract such strong-arm, unscrupulous tactics, given Mr Teixeira's connections with Mr Havelange, the project's advanced planning stage, the fact that I was about to start an uncertain fight for my own life, and the fact that Mr Machline's sons had a troubled business empire to take care of.'

Herson had intensive chemotherapy and regained his health. He says that he heard rumours that Teixeira and Coelho tried to launch the gambling business in France but it never got off the ground.

Herson ended his report to Blatter, 'The Brazilian press, eager to nail down Mr Teixeira, who has been embroiled in an endless series of allegations of misconduct, was eager to learn of the details of this huge project, but I was never interested in sharing this amazing, documented saga with the press, in deference to Mr Machline's memory.'

During the Senate corruption investigation Havelange was called to give evidence. He was asked whether he was one of those men 'who has made millions from football'.

'I challenge you to produce a document,' Havelange retorted. 'All I have done all my life is to work with dignity and respect.'

6

DASSLER'S BOYS LOSE THE OLYMPICS

... and need football more than ever

AFTER Horst Dassler's death in 1987, the family put his sister Sigrid's husband Christoph Malms at the top of the empire as president. Malms was on the short side, trim with cropped black hair. After Harvard Business School he'd gone to work at McKinsey, the management consultants full of bright young MBA's groomed to believe that 'anything you can do we can do better'. But were Harvard and McKinsey the best background for this peculiar industry? Many of the staff at ISL had doubts. Sports marketing was a people business complicated by raging egos, corruption and sometimes, bribes. Was Christoph really suited for it?

Expansion, he decided, was the future. ISL spread around the globe. The group's confidential organogram – a great diagrammatic map of ISL's world-wide operations including some based in Grand Cayman and the British Virgin Islands – grew to list

more than 60 companies. The impenetrable principality of Liech-
tenstein, squashed between Switzerland and Austria, played host
to two more companies, Lofa Football Establishment and Lofa
Establishment. Inquiries into these stopped at brass plates on
lawyers' doors in the capital, Vaduz.

Malms may have had the top title but it was Jean-Marie Weber
who went back to the early days of Horst Dassler and was
intimate with Havelange and Blatter. His job description was
'rights acquisitions and sports relations'. He schmoozed the sports
leaders and persuaded them to pass their precious marketing
rights to ISL, now based at the lakeside in Lucerne. Their offices
sat on top of the train station, amid the charming jumble of
painted ancient stone buildings, bierkellers and churches at the
water's edge.

Throughout 1995 the ISL salesmen looked again and again at
football and did their calculations over and again; how could more
money be wrung out of the game? They had squeezed as much
as the market would bear from sponsors. Jean-Marie Weber and
the Dassler family wanted more. Where could it come from?

In the past FIFA had sold the World Cup television rights to the
World TV consortium of public broadcasters with the European
Broadcasting Union leading the negotiations. After the 1994
World Cup in America ISL took apart the balance sheet of every
broadcaster that had bought rights to screen the tournament. They
added up how much money each company had earned from sell-
ing advertisements. They deducted how much had been paid to
FIFA for the rights to show the games – and they gasped.

The surplus was huge. Television companies were buying the
games low and selling the ads high and making vast profits
screening the World Cup. Jean-Marie Weber realised that FIFA
were giving the tournament away cheap. They should be charging
far more. This was a job for ISL.

It would be tough for public service networks like the BBC in Britain who didn't sell advertising, didn't make profits and had a duty to the public. But it was going to be wonderful news for Jean-Marie Weber and Joao Havelange and a great comfort after the disappointment of the fatal helicopter crash in New Jersey.

IN THE early winter of 1995, with ISL staffers still crunching FIFA's numbers, tall Jean-Marie Weber and short Christoph Malms flew to Japan for a routine business meeting about Olympic rights with the IOC. This piece of business was another part of Horst Dassler's legacy, the thank you from Juan Antonio Samaranch for inserting him into the Olympic presidency in 1980.

The Dassler family had treated their exclusive right to market the Olympics as a long-term investment. They started with the games in Seoul in 1988 just after Horst died and they lost money. They were in the red again in Barcelona in 1992 but in the mid-1990s looked ready to move into profit. By December 1995, Weber and Malms were about to tell the IOC that they'd signed up US$90 million worth of business with Coca-Cola and McDonald's and were close to a deal with Motorola and Shell oil. Wouldn't the IOC be pleased with all this money coming in, less of course ISL's 25 per cent commission?

But the IOC wasn't pleased. Weber and Malms were confronted in a hotel room by the IOC's hatchet-men, Director General Francois Carrard, senior member Dick Pound and Michael Payne, the former British skier who had worked for ISL before jumping ship to the IOC. They were brusque. We don't need you any more, they said. We're taking the business in-house. Goodbye.

Malms flew back to Zurich and an emergency board meeting shortly after lunch on 7 December 1995 in a room in Badenerstrasse borrowed from auditors KPMG. Christmas decorations glittered in shop windows, carols tinkled from loudspeakers but the five directors were deep in gloom. Sacked. By the IOC, of all people.

Perhaps the most anxious was Suzanne Dassler, who'd rushed from her lakeside home near Lausanne on the far side of the country. Short and dark and strongly built like her father, Suzanne, a shy woman, was proud of Horst's legacy and angered by people she thought might be trying to exploit it. She believed he had been a great innovator and she distrusted outsiders who were doing so well out of Dad.

Jean-Marie Weber didn't attend the emergency meeting. He'd spent years assuring the family that since Horst died he'd done a great job maintaining the strong personal ties with the IOC. The Olympic contract was safe in his hands, he'd said. He was fortunate to escape the Dasslers' fury that afternoon. Even through the stilted language of the confidential minutes you can sense the heartbreak. 'We have a duty to write to Mr Samaranch and tell him we do not appreciate what he is doing to us,' insisted Suzanne. The others hushed her. No independent actions, please. This must remain confidential and we need to have a coordinated strategy.

But they knew what rankled. Her father had discovered a little Catalan in jackboots and fascist blue shirt and repackaged him as the man of peace leading the IOC. Back in the 1980s after Horst had fixed the vote, Samaranch was happy to hand him the new marketing contracts. Where was the loyalty now?

What a bad day. It wasn't just a contract. The Olympics made ISL look the best, the cleanest, the most 'Olympian' of all the marketing companies in the sports business. For months they tried to stop the bad news leaking out.

They still had the rights to the World Athletics Championships and they turned a profit. But the big one, the richest one, that was about to get richer, the best contract in the world was the exclusive marketing and television rights to football. They must not lose those. The pressure was on Jean-Marie Weber.

FIFA EXECUTIVES say that Havelange and Blatter were genuinely shocked when Jean-Marie Weber turned up at the mansion on Sunny Hill and told them, *Listen carefully, never mind losing the gambling money, you never had it anyway, get your heads around this. Would you like to double your money from the World Cup? Treble it? How about 10 times as much? We're not talking millions, football's now in the billion dollar league . . .*

When the FIFA executives had absorbed the potential value of the television rights they realised the power this torrent of money would deliver. With a bulging bank account FIFA could help out every national association with money and new facilities. This would transform the world game and inevitably have the effect of entrenching the positions of those who had delivered such unprecedented growth. But would the financial controls you would usually find in a company with a balance-sheet of this kind ever be put in place by FIFA executives?

Weber was nervous. For nearly two decades, thanks to Horst Dassler's special relationship with Havelange, ISL had received the exclusive marketing rights to every World Cup as far ahead as 1998 in France. But not beyond. FIFA would have to offer the marketing and television rights to the 2002 World Cup to anyone who wanted to bid. Rivals would do the calculations and see how valuable the tournament had become. ISL might get beaten in an auction. Or win 2002 and lose next time around.

Maybe there was a solution that would save ISL's skin. *Secure a deal for more than one World Cup at a time.* But that possibility would have to be kept secret for as long as it could.

Let the rivals crunch their numbers on incomplete information. Let them arrange bank guarantees for too little. Keep them in the dark for as long as possible. But surely, this was impossible. You simply couldn't run a fair and open tendering process like that. Could you?

7

A STRANGE FIGHT FOR
THE WORLD CUP

Referee: Sepp Blatter

THERE was someone else who wanted the World Cup very badly and thought he knew how to get it: Eric Drossart, the elegant Belgian president in Europe of IMG, the American marketing company created in 1960 by Mark McCormack to exploit Arnold Palmer's golf swing and charm.

More golfers, and then tennis players, racing drivers, skiers, rock stars and fashion models joined the client list. IMG signed up baseball and basketball, cricket and rugby. They'd brought the television rights to Wimbledon, they looked after Oxford University, the Nobel Foundation, soccer clubs and Pelé. Mark McCormack's boys usually got what they wanted, outbidding all rivals. Now they wanted the football World Cup.

Eric Drossart had negotiated a partnership between IMG and UFA, the television subsidiary of Bertelsmann, the world's biggest media conglomerate. They went to their banks and obtained the guarantee letters needed to accompany a big-number bid.

Drossart opened his campaign on 18 August 1995 with a stunning offer. 'Dear Sepp,' he faxed, 'we are offering to pay US$1 billion for the World Cup 2002.' Knowing a bit about Sepp's special relationship with ISL, Drossart copied his offer to every single member of FIFA's executive committee.

You might have thought the offer of a thousand million dollars from two gold-plated companies would have made Blatter ecstatic. Quite the opposite. He was furious. 'We have to express our surprise at the way the letter to the General Secretary of FIFA was termed "strictly confidential" but copies were sent by telefax to all the members of the FIFA Executive Committee,' complained Blatter to Drossart. 'We are not convinced that this was the most suitable method of communicating a message of a confidential nature and it might have been more appropriate to have deleted this misnomer.'

Three weeks later Blatter wrote again to Drossart in London. He requested the details of the offer for 2002 alone. Notably, given what happened subsequently, he made no mention of 2006. Blatter said he wanted the information in less than one month, by mid-October. And he assured Drossart, 'FIFA are now busy arranging the timetable for the bid procedure.'

A month after that October 1995 deadline Blatter told Drossart and his billion dollars to wait for the next few months because Jean-Marie Weber had exclusive negotiating rights until 29 February 1996. 'We must respect these priority rights,' said FIFA's general secretary.

Drossart and his team at IMG weren't idle during the cold-shoulder waiting period. They met privately with Korean FIFA Vice-President Chung Mong-Joon, a son of the founder of the Hyundai dynasty, at the Sheraton at Frankfurt airport. A few days later they met with another Vice-President, African confederation President Issa Hayatou in Paris. They learned that the five continental presidents were pressing Havelange to set up a special committee to find out what was on offer, to make him and Blatter share information. But nothing was happening.

So Drossart made another dazzling offer: 'I want you to be aware of the fact that IMG/UFA are prepared to offer the most attractive bid to FIFA for the World Cup 2002 commercial rights, irrespective of alternative proposals.' An open-ended offer to blow all competition out of the water. The date was 7 December 1995, the very day that Dassler's traumatised family were in the ISL crisis meeting discussing what on earth they should do about losing the Olympics. They badly needed Blatter's help. Would he give it to them?

Blatter wrote once more to Drossart, just before the holidays. 'Best wishes for a merry Christmas and a happy New Year.' Then there was silence. The months fell off the calendar and on 15 March 1996, two weeks after the exclusive negotiating period with ISL had expired, Blatter wrote to Drossart. They were still talking with ISL, he wrote, and, regarding television rights, they'd only recently received 'a definitive offer for 2002 and beyond'. What was this 'and beyond?' Beyond what? All the talk for the past few years had been about a deal for 2002 only. What else might be on the table?

Blatter was promising 'transparency in the marketing of the World Cups'. *Cups?* How had this plural crept in? Was it a typing error? Drossart still didn't know when FIFA would talk to him about his offer.

Drossart learned more when he read the papers a few days later. Blatter put out a press statement on 19 March 1996 revealing not only was he still having private talks with ISL, he was also negotiating with the international television consortium of public broadcasting networks – known in the trade as the CCC. They had been major purchasers from FIFA for 1990, 1994 and the upcoming 1998 tournament in France at the old prices. It was hard to see how they could match Drossart's billion. Most puzzling was Blatter's claim that FIFA was 'scrutinising the offers submitted by other interested parties'. And here was that throwaway line again, a reference to offers for the 2002 World Cup and 'beyond'. But still no firm mention of 2006.

On 29 March Drossart sent another fax. 'We do not believe that the World Cup representation question is being dealt with evenly by FIFA.' Six months earlier 'you advised us that you were busy arranging the timetable for the bid procedure. We have never been told what the bid procedure is.' He went on, 'No negotiations or any sort of dialogue is taking place with us. Is this exclusion deliberate?' he asked Blatter. And what was this about rights for more than one World Cup being offered? 'We assume this is a level playing field and all bidders will be given the same information, bid document, and opportunity for negotiation, presentation etc,' said Drossart and concluded, 'You can rest assured that we will exhaust all possibilities to ensure that this process is dealt with on an even-handed basis.'

FIFA's general secretary waited nearly three weeks and then replied on 18 April. The rights to the World Cups of 2002 and 2006 were available as one package and if Drossart wanted to bid, he'd better get his finger out and submit a bid by 15 May. That left just 27 days for IMG's bid to be costed and guaranteed.

On 26 April, even as his numbers chaps were frantically crunching a new set of calculations covering two tournaments and raising another billion or more in bank guarantees, Drossart wrote to Sepp, 'I must admit that I am amazed by the content of your letter of 18 April. Whilst I welcome the apparent invitation from FIFA to be involved in the bid process for World Cup rights, there are glaring inconsistencies in your letters to us concerning the basis on which the rights are being made available and such obviously preferential treatment being given to other parties such as the CCC and ISL, that as of today it is difficult to believe that FIFA genuinely wish to consider our offer on a properly competitive basis.'

Near the end of this lengthy letter Drossart said bluntly, 'Sepp, it is very difficult to conclude anything other than there being two sets of rules in operation here ... and your responses to our efforts are merely a cosmetic exercise designed to protect FIFA from future accusations of unfair and improper competitive conduct.'

The bidding moved into the final phase. ISL had difficulties persuading their banks to underwrite their bid. Reluctantly they went to see Leo Kirch, the reclusive German television entrepreneur who had built up one of the biggest film libraries outside Hollywood and also had the rights to screen the best of German football.

The banks liked Leo and couldn't lend him enough. He had only one condition. 'I must have the World Cup rights for Germany,' said Leo and although it was one of the most prized territories, Jean-Marie had to agree. Leo pondered their request for a few minutes and then with the steely nerve that had made him a billionaire, the mogul from Munich said yes and ISL were back on track.

All bids were submitted on 15 May and Blatter locked them in his safe. Revised bids were submitted a month later and the executive committee would decide who got the business. But not all of the members appeared to know when the crucial meeting would be. UEFA president Lennart Johansson urged that FIFA's auditors should supervise the process.

The committee met on 5 July 1996, and on the agenda was what appeared to be a routine update for members on the television and marketing contracts. It was listed at point 3.1 as

'Report to the finance committee about award of the TV rights.' Havelange from the chair proposed that the rights for both 2002 and 2006 should go to the ISL and Leo Kirch consortium. He demanded that members make up their minds immediately. Havelange turned first to Russia's Viacheslav Koloskov. 'Are you not of the opinion we should accept the offer, my friend?' He blinked and said yes.

As Havelange went around the table, eyeballing member after member, Blatter kept count. Nine members agreed with Havelange, six voted against and three abstained. Absent from the meeting was the ageing billionaire Henry Fok from Hong Kong and Gerhard Mayer-Vorfelder. The German said later that he hadn't known such an important item was on the agenda.

Had Mayer-Vorfelder attended and voted against Jean-Marie Weber and Leo Kirch their bid would have died. Seven against plus the three abstentions would have outnumbered the nine favourable votes.

In July 1996, with all the bids in, the financial terms of the ISL/Kirch offer proved superior to those submitted by all other bidders. There was a further 18 months of negotiations on the marketing rights. In early September 1997 Jean-Marie Weber reported to his board that because of the 'delicate political situation' and to avoid a split in FIFA's executive committee the news that ISL had definitely won the marketing contract would be delayed while members could ask any questions. There was nothing to worry about. 'The members of the FIFA Executive Committees can ask questions, but cannot prevent the conclusion of the contract with ISL,' he reported gleefully. The minutes of the meeting record Christoph Malms congratulating Weber and his team.

*　　*　　*

FOUL!

THE SHOCKING statement from the bank that arrived in the basement mailroom at FIFA headquarters up on Sunny Hill that chilly winter morning in 1998 revealing the transfer of one million Swiss francs to a senior football official caused more than short-term consternation in the general secretary's corner office. Everybody in the finance department heard about it the same day. Word later spread through the building. It was a cock-up of mammoth proportions. But how had it happened?

A source familiar with the transaction explained to me later: 'It was a mistake by an ISL clerk who had been told to make a black payment to a senior football official who had helped them win the contract. Instead of sending the money direct to him, it went accidentally to FIFA. Before the end of the day the money had been forwarded to the football official.'

Five years later Eric Drossart told *Businessweek* magazine, 'The whole process was never explained, and when I made an offer, I would only receive vague answers.'

For this book I asked Drossart if he would care to say more. 'As you know, timing is of the utmost importance in life, and I believe the time when I would have been prepared to talk about the subjects you raise is long behind us,' he mused, 'and, as we say in French, it would now be considered *moutarde après le dîner*. I am now looking forward to helping my company secure new substantial deals (and more accessible!) across the board of the sports spectrum.'

8

EXIT HAVELANGE, FOOT IN MOUTH

Blatter moves into position

Nigeria, 8 November 1995. President Havelange took tea with Nigerian President Sani Abacha in his palace at Abuja. Havelange had a diplomatic problem. The World Youth Soccer Championships were soon to be held in Nigeria. That made Sani Abacha very glad. But there'd been outbreaks of cholera and meningitis. There was no way FIFA could fly teams of youths into Nigeria, and Sani Abacha felt sad about that. Havelange wanted to make him happy again. So he'd come to Nigeria for four days to ooze charm at the murderous, thieving dictator.

The world beyond the palace and the police state that Nigeria had become was concerned about something greater than Sani Abacha's disappointment over a football tournament. In Port Harcourt jail on Nigeria's coast, the executioners prepared the scaffold. It would need to be in tip-top condition for the killing of Ken Saro-Wiwa, a man who'd been bold enough to accuse the

Shell Oil company of waging 'ecological war' in the Niger River delta, homeland of his Ogoni people. He'd led non-violent protests against Shell and against Abacha's theft of the nation's oil wealth. Saro-Wiwa would die for his courage along with eight other dissenters unless someone could change Sani Abacha's mind.

Across the world decent people clamoured to stop the executions of men who'd become known as the 'Ogoni Nine'. The trials had been rigged, the men had been beaten. This was murder. Nelson Mandela had led the protests for months. Ambassadors were withdrawn. Plans were announced to suspend Nigeria from the British Commonwealth, trade sanctions were prepared, last-ditch appeals for mercy arrived from writers, artists, celebrities, from ordinary people all over the world. The executioners admired their work. The scaffold looked ready for action.

Inside the Abuja Palace, President Havelange and Sani Abacha sipped their tea and smiled. Havelange agreed that Nigeria could host the World Youth Soccer Championships in 1997. Sani Abacha was happy again. So happy that he appointed Havelange an honorary tribal chieftain. Havelange left the meeting and told the press, 'I feel honoured to be received and I am happy his Excellency has reiterated his desire to see the 1997 competition take place in Nigeria.'

Two days later the executioners rose early. Acting on Sani Abacha's orders they tied Ken Saro-Wiwa's hands behind his back and tightened the noose at his throat. Then they bungled it. It took five attempts but finally they snapped the bolt cleanly and Ken Saro-Wiwa's body dropped down, down, and came up sharply, neck broken, voice of dissent forever crushed. Next. It was a hard morning's work murdering the Ogoni Nine.

In one of his last, moving statements, Ken Saro-Wiwa had told the court, 'I am not one of those who shy away from protesting injustice and oppression, arguing that they are expected of a military regime. The military do not act alone. They are supported by a gaggle of politicians, lawyers, judges, academics and businessmen, all of them hiding under the claim that they are only doing their duty.'

He might have added, they are supported by the FIFA president too.

Cornered in Prague two days after the hangings Havelange said defiantly, 'I will not let politics affect my promise to award the 1997 World Youth Soccer Championships to Nigeria. Sport and politics should not be mixed.'

In London *The Sunday Times* accused Havelange of 'a one-man campaign to bring world football into disrepute ... while shock and anger have been expressed over the hangings, the FIFA president was sucking up to their military leaders.'

Two months later at the African Nations Cup in South Africa angry fans waved posters mourning the Ogoni Nine and damning Abacha. Their fury found no echo inside FIFA. For this was Planet Havelange. A world he had created in his image. It had a different scale of values. Still, Havelange had slipped up. He'd shown a lack of judgement. It was a matter of presentation. He'd made FIFA look bad, embracing Abacha so warmly. His position was weakened. Havelange should take care not to trip again.

He tripped again. And this time it mattered hugely to football. Havelange had allowed Japan and Korea to compete to stage the 2002 World Cup. Didn't he realise the depth of bitterness among Koreans? Japan had occupied their country for the first half of the twentieth century. As winter gave way to spring in 1996 the bickering between Japan and Korea was getting nasty. And FIFA was coming in for the blame. How could they be foolish enough to set up a contest in which one of these proud nations had to lose face?

In his arrogant way, Havelange had assured the Japanese that he could deliver the vote for them at FIFA's executive committee. But Korea was determined to win and they had a lot of backing on the committee. The bidding war surged aggressively. As spring gave way to summer the rumours of bribery took shape when FIFA vice-president David Will said he didn't want to be offered any more gifts. Will, a reserved lawyer from Scotland's chilly north-east, said he'd been offered everything except cash. You don't offer cash to David Will. That's not to say a few others weren't better off by the end of the campaign. One said of another, 'I know he takes bribes. I've had to pay him myself.'

Havelange was the last one to surrender to the obvious. FIFA couldn't wind the clock back. Only giving the tournament to both nations, permitting what FIFA had always said they didn't want, co-hosting, could prevent missiles flying across the Sea of Japan. It would be an organisational nightmare and his inept leadership was going to cost them a fortune. They'd need to pay for two of everything from now on.

Things just weren't going Havelange's way. And there was bitterness in the executive committee, especially among the Europeans, about the way Havelange and Blatter were handling the bidding for the rights to the World Cup of 2002 and 2006. IMG's Eric Drossart copied his furious letters to Blatter to every member of the committee.

Havelange and Blatter ignored Drossart and cold-shouldered the European members who took his side. They weren't happy and they took a little revenge. Denmark's Poul Hyldgaard was a Havelange man on the finance committee and he worked with Blatter supervising the war of the contracts. At their regional congress the European members savagely voted Hyldgaard out of his seat. Knifing Hyldgaard sent a message to Havelange.

Having seemed infallible for twenty years, Havelange's

dictatorial reign was disintegrating. He liked to make his own decisions, have them rubberstamped by the committee. They weren't going to do that anymore. He celebrated his 80th birthday on 29 May 1996. He knew it was time to go.

A SEAT ON FIFA's executive committee is among the most prized and best-rewarded positions in world sport and some soccer administrators will do anything in the hope of squeezing their bottoms on to one. It's a golden club and there are just 24 members.

It's not just the lavish expenses, the salary, first-class flights and swanky hotels to be enjoyed for the rest of their lives – even when they leave they'll get honorary membership, seats on committees and tickets for the World Cup, guaranteed all the way to the morgue. It's the power. Wealthy nations dropping to their knees begging to be given the World Cup tournament, the youth cups and the women's championships. So many people who have no other aim in life than be nice to you.

As FIFA's decision often hinges on which way a couple of votes will swing, you're a guest for every big match in the royal box or the president's stand. The big Merc whisks you through the hordes of fans trudging the last mile to the stadium. There've been so many objections to the extraordinary self-indulgence at the IOC yet few have noticed the holidays, gifts and all the goodies on offer to FIFA's magnificent 24.

In July 1996 FIFA held its two-yearly congress, in Zurich. On the agenda, a proposal to increase the size of the committee. There was huge excitement in the ranks. More seats meant more power. And there was one man in particular who was hungry for power.

You can hardly kick a ball against a wall between Georgetown,

Guyana, and the Arctic Circle without Jack Warner's permission and he'll expect a cut of the ticket and TV sales. He's a short, muscular man with a surprisingly squeaky, lisping voice. But when he speaks, people jump.

From the office in Port of Spain, Trinidad, that he owns and rents back to CONCACAF, the regional football confederation he controls, Warner fondly regards his thick wedge of the global soccer cake, stretching from the Atlantic to the Pacific. It gives him, automatically, a seat in FIFA's golden club, the executive committee. Most of his members come from tiny Caribbean islands, where the only professional soccer is beamed in by satellite from Europe. There's so many islands that his confederation qualifies for three executive committee seats.

Zurich, Kongresshaus, 4 July 1996. It wasn't easy getting through from Port au Prince but finally Dr Jean-Marie Kyss, president of Haiti's football association, got a connection to Caribbean football officials who'd already arrived in Zurich for the congress. 'I won't be coming,' he told them. 'The post is so slow, the invitation has just arrived, we're short of money and we've got a Cuban team visiting so, what with one thing and another, we'll pass.'

Damn doctor Kyss! There goes a precious vote. The delegate has to be there. But then, who knows Dr Kyss? He's just a doctor in the Port au Prince slums. No-one outside Jack Warner's obedient continental federation would recognise Kyss. Let's find someone to vote in his place.

It couldn't be a European, an Asian or an Arab. And every available African was already wearing credentials. Warner hadn't brought any spare Caribbean men with him. They'd all been named and listed. He could hardly send one of his retinue back into the lobby stuttering, 'Sorry, I was drunk when I arrived, I got my name wrong. Actually I'm a soccer official from Haiti – bonjour – can I have my accreditation please?' Even the gaggle of cowed Blatter staffers handing out delegate badges couldn't let that pass.

And then clickety-clack, the required dark skin, all heels and no-accreditation person – the wrong sex, but who cares? – came shimmying through the crowds. Yes, she'd do fine, Vincy Jalal, the girlfriend of Jamaica's football president Horace Burrell. She'd come along for the fun of a trip to Europe, a few nights' rumpy-pumpy in a five-star bed, some boutique hopping and a glimpse of the Alps. They called Horace the Captain, because he'd been an officer in the Jamaican Defence Force, he loved his rank and the image that went with it. Yes, the Captain's lady would be perfect.

A quick call to FIFA's head of credentials. Dr Kyss had dropped out long ago, Haiti's sent a replacement, V Jalal, and Jack had got his vote back. Who cared that she was one of only half a dozen women amongst a thousand men? Hadn't general secretary Blatter said that women were the future of football? She took her place near the centre of the hall at Haiti's table, in time for the roll-call. FIFA seats its delegations in alphabetical order, Albania and Angola at the front, Uganda and Ukraine at the rear. Seated next to Vincy Jalal was Guyana, represented by Jack's close ally Colin Klass, and a few tables away was Jamaica from where the good Captain Horace could toss billets-doux, blow kisses and whisper words of advice to this novice in FIFA procedures.

There were 44 delegates in the hall from Jack and Horace's region, the Confederation of North, Central America and Caribbean Association Football and they'd all been together three months earlier in Guadalajara in Mexico for their own congress. Most knew the men from Haiti but not one of them wondered aloud how the place of the quietly spoken and reserved grey-haired, bespectacled Dr Kyss had been taken by an eye-catching babe.

General secretary Sepp Blatter started the roll-call. Vincy's an English speaker but when 'Haiti?' was called, she did her best to deliver a firm 'Oui'. The voters were welcomed to Zurich by Marcel Mathier, president of the Swiss FA, chairman of FIFA's Disciplinary Commission and the guardian of football's morals.

When the resolution that could give Jack Warner another seat for his continent came up for debate, the vote was called and Vincy got up from her seat, click-clacked to the front, showed her credentials, took Haiti's voting slip, went to the booth and, behind the curtains, voted the way Burrell told her to. Vincy's attendance proved to be a waste of time. Jack didn't get his extra seat.

IOC president Juan Antonio Samaranch graciously accepted FIFA's Congress Gold Medal and praised his hosts. 'Examples set in the deliberations taking place would be closely watched and emulated by other sports federations,' he said. FIFA's Order of Merit was awarded to businessman Robert Louis-Dreyfus who'd bought Adidas, Doug Ivester of fellow sponsors Coke and Henry Kissinger.

As he came to the end of a speech examining his 22 years in power, and finding his conduct nothing less than admirable, Havelange sprang his great surprise. Happy days were just around the corner. Every one of the national associations would from 1999 be given a million dollars every four years, thanks to ISL, 'our partners and friends'.

Where would this cash windfall come from? Television networks were going to pay more than ever before to screen the World Cup. Everybody was going get rich.

The record of the meeting was checked and approved by five

FIFA member countries, including Jamaica and Switzerland. That official record will show forever, near the bottom right-hand corner of page six, that although Dr Kyss stayed at home, Haiti did have a delegate whose name, misspelt, was 'Julal Vincy'. After the Captain and his lady had retired for the night and the rum began to flow there were a few laughs at her expense among some of the braver Caribbean delegates. Ever since, but only when Jack and Horace aren't in earshot, Ms Vincy Jalal has been known as 'Ms Oui'.

AT THE END of 1996, in the first week of December, Havelange wrote to every member of the committee, reminding them of the special dinner they had given for him and his wife Anna Marie on his birthday. 'That evening will remain unforgettable for me,' he said, 'since it symbolises the warmth of your friendship.' FIFA and its continents were in a blessed state of unity and, 'convinced that I have fulfilled my mission' he would not run again in 1998. Who would replace him?

LENNART JOHANSSON started work at the bottom of a large industrial flooring company and rose to the top. He made his way from the grassroots of Swedish soccer to lead the national federation. He climbed upwards through UEFA and when they made him president in 1990 he automatically became a FIFA vice-president. Johansson was a man moulded by sport rather than politics. His Scandinavian low-church upbringing gave him an allegiance to democracy and openness that set him apart from trefoil-branded politicos like Havelange and Blatter.

Politely, when Havelange announced his retirement, he waited for nine months and then in September 1997, surrounded by

European soccer leaders in Helsinki, Johansson said he would run for the presidency. That left another nine months until the Paris congress in June 1998, on the eve of the next World Cup.

Johansson, at 69, a big lumbering, jowly bear of a man with greying hair produced a reform programme. He promised democracy, solidarity and transparency. But that wasn't good news to some people. In his solid, thoughtful, choose-every-word-carefully manner, Johansson said that if elected, 'I will push for an independent accountant to examine FIFA's business practices.'

Johansson produced a campaign brochure and in it he claimed the support of IOC President Juan Antonio Samaranch, Pelé, Sir Bobby Charlton and Franz Beckenbauer. It was all very impressive but none of them had a vote.

Johansson's Mr Clean campaign needled Havelange. How dare he call for independent investigations? Havelange had no affection for Blatter; hadn't the man tried to unseat him? But there was one thing going for Sepp. He might call for transparency but there was no danger that he'd actually open the shutters and let some light in. So Havelange's secrets might stay safe in a FIFA ruled by President Blatter.

Meanwhile Blatter sat tight up on Sunny Hill talking, talking all the time on the phone to football officials around the world. He could have spoken firmly to more than half of the national associations, and demand they repaid loans outstanding to Zurich – but he didn't. Given the chance, they'd want to thank him for this, they could see what kind of friendly president he would make.

In early December FIFA and the coaches and journalists from the 32 countries that had qualified for the French World Cup met in Marseille for the final draw. Havelange mentioned casually that Blatter had 'all the qualities to be the president'. But Blatter wasn't running. At least, not openly.

Christmas passed, election year commenced and Blatter rarely left his office. After 17 years as chief bureaucrat in Zurich he knew when old friendships could be profitably renewed and new friends made. One frantic period was at the beginning of a World Cup year. In 1998 the magic date was 15 January, the closing day for FIFA insiders to place orders for tickets, ahead of them going on general sale.

It was a time when the venal would whack in vast orders for resale to touts, brokers and package tour operators. Perhaps the scoundrels believed Blatter would be disinclined to say 'No' to anybody this year. Some general secretaries of national associations ordered tickets.

Chet Greene from tiny Antigua faxed his order direct to 'The General Secretary, FIFA House, Switzerland', although it's not known whether the General Secretary himself ever saw it. His demand came in the name of the Antigua and Barbuda FA. Attached to his covering letter were three sheets listing every one of the 64 matches between the first round and the Final. He wanted 47 tickets for the Brazil–Scotland opening game, hundreds more for other games and 147 tickets for the final. Chet Greene's total order was for 2,964 tickets.

Havelange made another carefully timed interjection that he thought Blatter would make an 'outstanding' president.

Blatter had nothing to gain from openly declaring his candidacy. The longer he procrastinated, the longer he could continue as general secretary in the control room of the sprawling organisation, manipulating the power and patronage at his disposal. Johansson was the challenger, Blatter was effectively the heir apparent.

He put it about that he hadn't made up his mind. 'However, if one or several federations wish to nominate me then I will make up my mind,' he said. 'You're not credible,' taunted Italian vice-president Antonio Matarrese, Johansson's first lieutenant and UEFA's attack dog.

Despite the ticket rackets and debt forgiveness, courtesy of Blatter, Johansson was making solid gains. In February he pitched his reforms to a meeting of the leaders of the African Football Confederation in little Burkina Faso, sandwiched between Mali and Ghana. They promised that the votes of all Africa's 44 nations would be cast in one block for him. As president of UEFA, Johansson could expect nearly 50 European votes automatically and with Africa and the promises from East Asia he was confident of the support of more than half of the 200 or so national associations.

The election was drawing closer and still Blatter hadn't declared. The weeks were ticking down and with no announcement, no campaign and no rival programme to attack, Johansson was frustrated. His allies on the executive committee forced a meeting in mid-March in Zurich with one topic on the agenda: What were Blatter's intentions?

They simply couldn't allow him to be an undeclared candidate using his general secretary's power and influence to win votes. This time they figured they had him cornered. *Here are the options. Announce your candidacy and resign your job. Or tell us you're not running for president. If you equivocate, we'll suspend you.*

Blatter could expect 14 of the 24 voters to be hostile to him when the meeting began on the morning of 13 March under the gilt and chandeliers of a salon in the Dolder Grand Hotel. Havelange tried to seize the initiative, proposing that it was acceptable for Blatter to continue as general secretary, as long as he operated under certain unspecified constraints.

Member after member tried to extract from Blatter a clear statement of intent. *Speak up, no more prevaricating, are you or are you not a candidate?* Each time Blatter inspected his finger-nails, shuffled his pens, adjusted his tie, gazed out of the window. Time and again Havelange squashed the questioner. After four exhausting hours the Europeans had had enough. *Let's put it to vote*, they said. For the first time in 24 years of chairing FIFA's executive committee Havelange was going to suffer a defeat. He'd never been outvoted. What would he do?

'Everybody was stunned,' Scotland's David Will said later, in the hotel lobby. He's a moderate man, a silver-haired lawyer, but there was fury in his quiet clipped tones. 'A majority of the executive committee wanted Blatter to resign. At that point Dr Havelange and Mr Blatter walked out of the meeting and we were prevented from taking a vote.'

Havelange compounded the Europeans' fury by summoning the press and claiming that he had adjourned the meeting because they couldn't agree. 'I have to abide by the laws of this country,' he said bafflingly, 'and if there was a doubt, there was no point in proceeding.' Having bullied, baffled and bamboozled, Havelange turned on the charm. 'Many general secretaries have followed their presidents into office, why should it be so different at FIFA?'

THE KING IS DEAD, LONG LIVE THE KING

Blatter delivers the money

Paris, 30 March 1998. Blatter delayed two more weeks, out of sight and range of Johansson's artillery, then chose Paris on a Monday to announce that he'd been begged to run by several national associations including Australia, Brazil, Saudi Arabia, Jamaica, Trinidad, the USA and France. 'I am a servant of football and I will try to be as good a servant to football in the future,' he told the press. At his side was Michel Platini, now as hungry for success in football politics as he had been hungry for goals for France and Juventus. All curls and charisma, Platini was Blatter's choice to fill a new position, FIFA's Director of Sport. Blatter planned to be both president and continue as chief executive.

Platini, taking time off from his day job organising the World Cup, just weeks away, told journalists that he did not believe

FIFA was run democratically and feared that if Johansson won the election there would be no change. 'I have absolutely no personal interest,' he added. 'I'm a man of conviction and if I do this it's because I think I'm the only person who can get FIFA to change course because I was a player and a coach.'

Blatter promised to expand the executive committee. Places would be guaranteed for women. For referees. For players. Anybody who might get him a headline. When he won he would have to be paid but his salary would, and here emerged a word that he would often return to, be 'transparent'.

As well as being utterly transparent Blatter was going to protect soccer from 'exploitation by commercial and political forces'. An aide posted on Blatter's internet site the assertion: 'The success and standing of football in the world today can to a large degree be attributed to Joseph Blatter.'

Johansson braced himself for a dirty campaign. 'I am afraid that what has transpired until now will continue,' he said, 'that one will be confronted with things that are not acceptable from an ethical, moral and legal standpoint.'

Kigali, 5 April 1998. Havelange touched down in Rwanda, ostensibly to honour the nearly one million people slaughtered in the genocide four years before. Once that was out of the way, there was important work to be done. Havelange used the occasion to buttonhole officials who'd come from 17 East and Central African football associations to join the anniversary gathering. The crucial message: *Blatter is the man to support.*

Back in Zurich, Havelange wasted no time. He dictated a letter to his secretary, Marie-Madeleine Urlacher. The recipient, a Somali official. 'I should like to tell you how happy I was to see you in Kigali where you were able to expound your Federation's point of view,' smoothed Havelange. He said he was looking forward to greeting two Somali officials at the coming Paris congress, one funded by FIFA, 'and the other, as I promised you, will be my responsibility, as well as the cost of accommodation'. Football in East Africa was so dear to his heart that 'As to your national association, I have had a meeting with the FIFA Deputy General Secretary, Michel Zen-Ruffinen, concerning your development.' He promised technical seminars for referees, doctors and administrators. And he'd fly two lucky officials to Brazil for more courses.

Coincidentally, postmen and delivery drivers in Nairobi, Khartoum and Kampala were suddenly laden with gifts for the region's football decision makers, signed, with warm regards, from their dear friend Joao. Fax machines and photocopiers were wrapped and despatched to offices across Africa. Every nation represented at Kigali got one. In case that wasn't enough to swing the votes of the region Havelange instructed finance director Erwin Schmid to send one regional official a cheque for US$50,000. All Erwin needed was the name and number of a bank account. Havelange didn't bother to get approval from the finance committee. Why should he? He was the president.

Another letter went to the fabulous Fok family of Hong Kong. It was addressed to the billionaire Timothy, president of the local football association, a man with strong influence in Asian sport and soon to join the International Olympic Committee. Tim's dad Henry, who made one of his fortunes out of gambling in Macau, was scheduled to receive FIFA's Order of Merit in Paris. 'My dear friend President Timothy,' cooed the FIFA president, 'I seek your support for Mr Blatter.' Could Timothy deliver the votes of Hong Kong, Macau, China and North Korea? Havelange was especially concerned because he knew that Johansson was at that moment lobbying in China and the fabulous Foks, well-connected in Beijing, were the best hope of chopping him down.

Dublin, 30 April 1998. Havelange was in the enemy's camp. The season of the continental congresses had begun and the Europeans met at Jury's Hotel. The day was all about boosting Johansson. Blatter, the rival candidate, had not made the trip. This was not the time and place to drive a wedge through Europe. Havelange sat in the gloom of the auditorium's front row, peering up to the brightly lit stage where they celebrated Lennart Johansson, the man they hoped would replace him in six weeks time at the pinnacle of world football. The tributes went on and on.

At last they called Havelange to the platform and a UEFA official clipped their diamond pin of merit to his lapel. They said it was for his services to football but in truth it was a goodbye-and-good-riddance award.

Europe's treasurer was the amiable German, Egidius Braun. Chirruping like a happy sparrow at the podium, he reminded everyone of UEFA's financial aid to Eastern Europe (are you new guys at the back listening? Remember kindly Mr Johansson when you go to the ballot box in Paris). Havelange chewed on a piece of gum. When the two big screens above the stage flashed alive with Braun's financial report featuring lots of lovely Swiss francs Havelange perked up. Not for long. Having caught the old man's attention, Mr Braun chided that in the new world of honesty after the FIFA Congress, 'there must be no second cashbox – as they say in Switzerland!'

There was another ambush coming. The big screens lit up with Pelé, Johansson's number one fan and enemy of Havelange. He made a political speech with cheeky smiles. 'I have met many

Kings and Queens, presidents and stars in my travels around the world,' he beamed into the camera. 'But I have never met anyone who cares more for the honesty and transparency of the sport of football as my friend Johansson. I hope deeply in my heart that he becomes the next president of FIFA.'

The congress closed with a last burst of applause for Johansson, Havelange rocketed out of his seat and, more sprightly than any 82-year-old should be, he moved through the delegates to the back of the hall. He saw an old friend and paused. They muttered briefly and then he was off down the corridor, moving relentlessly through the crowds. Breathless, I scrambled my way through the melée, I nearly caught him in the hotel lobby but he was out in the car park already, climbing into Dublin's biggest rental Mercedes and speeding away into the late afternoon spring sunshine up Pembroke Road.

THE RIVALS circled the globe, their wingtips nearly touching as they tried to filch each other's support. Another two weeks on and Blatter and Johansson were in Kuala Lumpur for the congress of the Asian federation. Blatter told them that Europe and Africa were divided and that he would win. Johansson said he had received written pledges of support from 50 of the 51 European associations, at least 60 more worldwide, and he called Blatter's claim wishful thinking.

Blatter has the raw energy and instinct of a professional survivor, scanning a room in seconds to beam friendly glances to faces he knows, even if there's no love lost between them. Johansson is from a more gentlemanly background; football is a family and you shouldn't be rude about a cousin, even if they have spent the last six months trying to shaft you.

He nearly let himself go in Kuala Lumpur. 'Havelange is not

neutral. He even puts words in my mouth, which is wrong. He is not using truth, and this is very alarming to me.' Then Johansson pulled himself up, half-ashamed. 'I have tried to keep quiet about it, but sometimes it becomes too much.' Was this the first time his aides saw the possibility of defeat, suspected Lennart wasn't ruthless enough? Was he naïve to trust that all those written pledges would turn into votes?

Nairobi, 20 May 1998. It began as a dot in the sky but in less than a minute it took the shape of a small charter jet coming towards them from the south, from the Golden City. The eager football officials at the airport shaded their eyes in the African May morning sunshine. They made their way to the tarmac as the jet taxied towards the Nairobi terminal building. The engines stopped, the door opened and here he was, Mr Blatter, fresh in from Jo'burg, all waves and warm smiles, confident he could remember the names that his onboard briefers said would be ready to greet, shake hands, hug and think again about the precious votes they had promised to his rival.

Blatter flew in with joy in his heart. He'd had meetings with officials from South Africa, Mozambique, Angola, Lesotho and Namibia, five votes. He'd promised them that with his backing South Africa would host the World Cup in 2006. If he won he'd pump even more money into the continent. His audience liked what they heard from him in public and in private. That was five votes wrested from Johansson who was backing Germany for 2006. In Kigali Havelange had begun picking apart the block vote promised by African football's leadership back in February. Blatter was picking off more. Africa was splitting.

Coming off the plane behind Blatter were his persuaders, the tight, ruthless team determined to change minds in Africa. Right behind Blatter was his daughter Corinne. Next was Emmanuel Maradas, a big shaven-headed man from sub-Saharan Chad. Emmanuel was Blatter's occasional press spokesman. He was based in North London, married to Nim Caswell, sports editor of the *Financial Times*, and together they published the monthly *African Soccer Magazine*.

Jean-Marie Weber's ISL company bought pages of expensive advertisements in the magazine and the couple were familiar guests on the well-padded FIFA circuit. Blatter and Havelange were frequently the targets of attacks in newspapers around the world but Nim and Emmanuel tended to take a kinder view. In his luggage Emmanuel was carting copies of *African Soccer Magazine* and its May editorial 'Divided Loyalties' giving comfort to those who might want to vote for Blatter.

Last down the steps was the young Swiss lawyer Flavio Battaini. This was odd. Shouldn't he have been behind his FIFA desk in Zurich? What was he doing, risking his lawyerly reputation for neutrality by being seen in one of the rival camps? When Blatter finally declared he was a candidate he was forced to retreat from Sunny Hill and run his campaign from his spacious top-floor apartment in Zollikon with its views over Lake Zurich. He had given his word he would not take advantage of the organisation's funds, equipment or personnel. But his ever-loyal secretary Helen Petermann, from her office, next to Blatter's now empty one on the first floor, had drafted and dispatched the fax calling today's Nairobi meeting.

There'd been allegations that Blatter was improperly using FIFA's money and resources for his campaign and that was a lie and he wanted to squash it, urgently, immediately he landed in Nairobi. Blatter summoned the local reporters waiting at the airport, looked them in the eye, and, as one of them wrote, *vehemently* insisted, 'No travelling expenses, faxing, couriers, cell phone. Not a penny! All I have from FIFA is moral support!'

Now it was time to lobby the officials from Kenya, Uganda, Tanzania, Zanzibar, Somalia, Ethiopia and Sudan, the East and Central region of Africa.

The African officials were too canny to endorse Blatter immediately. They wanted to see what more Johansson might offer. Even so, Blatter said, 'I feel tremendously positive' and a dozen hours after he landed at Jomo Kenyatta airport, he was up in the air again, on the way back to Sunny Hill. The next day the headline in the *East African Standard* summed up Blatter's visit: 'BIG MONEY PROMISED.'

So, how was the now unemployed Mr Blatter paying for his costly campaign, hiring charter jets to hop around the world, entertaining at classy hotels, promising free trips to Paris, rarely off his cell-phone? His rival Johansson was given US$534,000 by UEFA and he told reporters, 'The executive committee approved this. All the details are open, they are all public, there is nothing to hide.'

Blatter told one reporter he had only US$135,000 to spend, then he informed another that actually his budget was US$300,000. Later, in a throwaway line, Blatter mentioned he had 'a few minor sponsors', the seriously rich Mohamed Bin Hammam from the fabulously wealthy oil and gas statelet of Qatar, for one. A few days before the election Blatter said, 'I have nearly run out of money. Michel Platini has graciously said he will foot the bill for the few drinks and refreshments we are going to have this morning.'

Platini took up the theme. 'What does FIFA mean to today's players? Nothing. The people they see are figureheads, staying in five-star hotels and eating in expensive restaurants. We want to change that.' Platini was talking with a reporter from the Associated Press who noted, deadpan, 'Platini's organising committee paid for the news conference, held in a meeting room of a four-star hotel and offering champagne and ritzy hors d'oeurves afterwards.'

'THEY OFFERED me US$100,000 to switch my vote from Johansson to Blatter ... Half in cash and the rest in football equipment for my country!' Once the lean man from Mogadishu in his white skull cap and gold-rimmed glasses started talking about the 1998 election he didn't stop for an hour. He was Farah Addo, Vice-President of African football. 'When I said no, I will not change my vote, they said OK, but we want you to influence the others. They thought I was stupid.'

Suddenly it was worth the two-day wait in the pink-dusty heat of Mali, watching the big trucks rumbling out in the cooler night to Timbuktu. It seemed that nearly every official at the African Nations Cup in January 2002 wanted an appointment with Farah Addo, once an international referee and now an influential football politician, and I was at the back of the queue. Addo held court in a sparsely furnished whitewashed office in a squat two-storey building in Bamako, across the road from the broad, slow-moving Niger.

Addo, flanked by officials in flowing robes from around the continent, made his points with vigour, his thin moustache flying up and down. He told how he took a call in his Cairo office from a former Somalian ambassador. It was troubling. The man was calling from a Gulf country. He was acting as a middleman. He was offering a bribe, US$100,000, if Addo would vote for Blatter. They especially wanted to get Addo aboard Sepp's campaign because he was also president of the Central and East African confederation and might influence more than a dozen votes.

Addo sent them packing and thought little more about it until he got to Paris and received a shock. 'When I reached the Montparnasse hotel my name was not there as President of the Somali Football Federation. It was not at the counter where you got credentials. But I had a copy of my original application for accreditation.' Addo lobbied the leaders of African and European football. 'They went to the leadership of FIFA, telling them they would make a scandal if my right to vote was not restored.' He got his vote back. Addo makes it clear that he has no proof that Blatter was involved in or had any knowledge of the attempt to bribe him or of the attempt to remove his vote.

Addo's claims that he was offered a massive bribe to sway votes to Blatter were amplified by former Somali officials who claimed they had been given a mixture of cash, air tickets and expenses to go to Paris. Some said the man behind the inducements was Mohamed Bin Hammam.

Bin Hammam is a small, slim man in his mid-fifties with a receding cap of flat, tight curls. He's quick to smile and quick to order coffee when we meet but come a point of disagreement his eyes suddenly narrow and his thin moustache twists as he curls his upper lip in disdain. Perhaps he's not used to being argued with, accustomed as he is to the respect of his half-a-pace-behind-him-eyes-averted entourage of bag carriers and bill settlers. His clothes are conservative and whether close-fitting dark suits or white silk jalabiyyas, look as if they engrossed a tailor for many months of delicate stitching.

He's not just rich. He is one of a select band of 35 men who sit on Qatar's Advisory Council, handpicked by absolute monarch Emir Hamad bin Khalifa Al Thani. A member of FIFA's cabinet since 1996, Bin Hammam is one of the Emir's favourites. His high profile in world football politics brings sporting status to a tiny country that pays big money to ageing foreign stars to play out the twilight of their careers in the local league. Out of season Qatar pays fortunes to young African runners to switch nationality and win medals for their new country.

When the bribery allegations began to fly, Bin Hammam produced a lengthy rebuttal. He didn't think anything wrong had happened in 1998. 'It is regrettable to see what we believed to be a fair contest and duel between knights, has now changed to a dirty war: I helped Mr Blatter immensely in his campaign in the 1998 election and some even claimed that I was the major reason for his victory not because I bribed people but because we planned the battle. We were right in the field while the others were sitting behind their desk.'

Bin Hammam revealed the personal cost of backing Blatter. 'We were in Paris and were planning a trip to South Africa in a commercial flight, not belonging to or financed by HRH the Emir of Qatar. The night before we travelled I received a frantic call from my wife with the shocking sad news that my son aged 22 years had met with a very serious accident and was fighting for his life and his condition was more towards death and was lying in the intensive care unit in a coma. I should immediately return to Doha. I regretted and apologised to my wife, and told her that my son doesn't need me but needs the blessing of God and help of doctors while it is Mr Blatter who is in need of my help now. So I sacrificed seeing my son maybe for the last time.'

Lennart Johansson and Michel Zen-Ruffinen, then FIFA general secretary, confirmed to me that Addo's 1998 congress registration documents had been altered to exclude him from voting, although they did not say by whom. They said they had insisted his accreditation was returned to him. Addo later asserted that at least 18 African officials, although publicly committed to Johansson, had sold their country's votes to supporters of Blatter. That would be enough to swing the result. If claims by Addo and others are true, then Blatter is an illegitimate president and Johansson was robbed.

At the end of 1998 Blatter was confronted by a Swiss reporter with the allegation that Qatar had provided the money for his expensive campaign. This he denied, retorting, 'The Emir gave me his plane only once for a flight from Paris to Dakar.' Blatter insisted that he had paid all his own election expenses.

Some time later in 2003, after I had asked Bin Hammam about the specific allegations, he invited me on an all-expenses paid trip to Qatar as his personal guest. 'I hope that you will accept my invitation,' he wrote, 'so I can send the air ticket to your address.'

For a moment I imagined life as it might be for a foot-soldier in the world of FIFA politics. A super-rich and famous man likes me. He wants to take me on a trip. He'll send tickets to my home. Kind hospitality. Sumptuous hotels. Perhaps he'll give me pocket money.

I pinched myself and politely declined his invitation.

DAYLIGHT ROBBERY *AGAIN*

How they stole the vote in Paris

DR JEAN-MARIE KYSS completes the morning's obstetric consultations for the impoverished women who come to the single-storey Centre Médical O. Durand in the pungent downtown streets of Port au Prince. Then from behind his desk overflowing with patients' files, he tells me about the problems he'd had trying to attend FIFA congresses. 'Soccer is big in Haiti,' he explains, 'and in the 1990s it generated a lot of cash at the turnstiles of our national stadium. First of all the government tried to steal it by imposing its own people on our federation. When that didn't work they tried to seize the stadium itself. The Secretary for Sport sent police and security men. Come and see it for yourself.'

Four years earlier in June 1998 as FIFA slithered towards its congress, the money was flowing again into the Stade Sylvio Cator. Closed for five years during another of Haiti's periods of violent upheaval it had recently reopened with a morale-boosting 3–0 trouncing of Martinique by the home team. For the poorest nation in the Western hemisphere, any kind of victory was sublime. So was the rattle of the cashbox to the crooks in the government.

Now, in the spring of 2002, grey-haired Kyss, in his neatly pressed but threadbare dark suit, was no longer president of the Haitian federation. He still didn't know what had happened at that FIFA congress back in 1996 in Zurich. Nobody had ever had the courage to tell him that his vote had been stolen by a gorgeous stand-in. But he *thought* he knew what happened in 1998.

We picked our way along half a dozen hot, crowded streets, around the market women, the motorbikes and piles of garbage, through the stadium gates, the tunnel and onto the brown pitch. Kyss is a well-loved man; there were smiles and waves from the ground staff. 'The clubs were behind me in 1998,' he said. As for the crooks in the government, 'eventually we beat them in the parliament and in the courts. So it seemed a good time to go to the congress in Paris.' But the thieves kept up the pressure.

'I and my wife Nicole went to the airport but when we got to the immigration control somebody told me, "The Doctor is not supposed to leave the country." I asked, "Have I committed any crime, have I violated any law?" They said it was the order of the Secretary of Sport. We had to stay in Haiti because there was no way we could get on the plane.'

Kyss had fought a brave battle to protect football in his own country but he couldn't argue with the gunmen at the airport. He put his passport in his pocket and walked away.

Kyss went back to his consulting rooms and started calling Paris, trying to reach officials of CONCACAF, the Caribbean and North American soccer confederation. 'I spoke to secretary Chuck Blazer and president Jack Warner. I explained to Mr Warner what had happened and told him that Haiti would not be represented at the FIFA congress. FIFA's rules do not allow proxy voting but

I would not want to mandate anyone to sit in our seat in Paris. That empty chair symbolised the interference of our government in our sport. It was our gesture of defiance. That empty chair sent a powerful message to the world.'

Sadly for Kyss, Jack Warner had other plans.

Paris, 8 June 1998. Football's parliament, the Congress, met to elect its new president. This was FIFA's most important day in 24 years, the first presidential election since Havelange outwitted Rous at the Frankfurt Kongresshalle. It was a sunny morning on the south side of the city and Lennart Johansson and half a dozen aides strolled along a narrow tree-lined street through crowds of reporters and cameramen to the Salle Equinoxe, an austere metal-clad assembly hall in an ugly exhibition complex. The reporters called to him and Johansson smiled back. He looked to have recovered from the late betrayal of the English. They'd switched their vote to Blatter in the hope that he'd bring the 2006 World Cup to England.

Blatter had been delighted, saying, 'The fact that England, the motherland of football, has come out so strongly to back me has touched me like nothing else in my campaign.' Johansson, glum, said 'a week ago the chairman of the English FA, Mr Keith Wiseman, told me they would be voting for me. Clearly they can no longer be trusted.' After the Heysel stadium disaster when 39 Juventus fans died, England had been banned from Europe and it was Johansson who'd got them back in. How soon they'd forgotten.

Johansson's worry had to be, who else would break ranks in Europe, his power base? First the French, now the English. His prediction of a lead on the first round followed by victory in the run-off was looking shakier.

Here was someone who must be important. Gliding up to the kerb was an extra-long Merc, flanked by running men in suits with government haircuts, curly wires coming out of their ears, and bulky lumps under their jackets.

A glimpse of robes in the back; it was Prince Faisal of Saudi Arabia. Prince Faisal was a member of the International Olympic Committee but he habitually missed their meetings and Games. Any other member would be cautioned, then expelled. Not a Saudi prince. So why had he and his sharp-eyed bodyguards made the journey here this Monday morning?

The Prince was going to cast a vote. Something no-one is allowed to do back home in undemocratic Saudi. Bring up that topic over sugared mint tea in the souk and your next public appearance may be in Riyadh's Chop Square. But the wealthy Prince was a great supporter of Blatter and keen to help lever him into power. It would be risking death by a dozen bullets to get near enough to ask him a question but one African official, Mr 'Bomba' Mthethwa, had told the *Swaziland Times* that his expenses had been paid by someone from the Middle East. He declined to name them, saying it might have 'a negative impact'.

Havelange conducted his final congress with his usual grace. The charisma that charmed enough voters to eject Sir Stanley Rous all those years ago had not dimmed, only matured. He still had that noble bearing. His penetrating eyes were sharp as ever. But they were set deeper in their sockets and looked darker; from some angles there was something of the night about him. Henry Fok stepped up to get his Order of Merit, a South African diplomat stood in for Mandela, England's Sir Bert Millichip got his. Then Havelange, well practiced at his own valedictories, delivered over the past couple of years, described himself as an 'idealist and visionary' and took credit for thinking up the idea of selling marketing and television rights.

He talked wistfully of his sponsors, the good people who made him what he was today: 'The collaboration of Coca-Cola and Adidas in the youth development programme and in youth competitions stems solely from a mutual desire to invest in youth and to create personal contacts and exchange of ideas beneficial to the "Planet Football".' Elsewhere on his planet, football was in trouble.

Havelange sat down to the applause he expected, the congress dealt with a few procedural matters and then moved to the election. Tension rose. The candidates, according to protocol, left the hall before the ballot. Johansson looked confident. For all Blatter's posturing, enough voters, especially the Africans, had looked Lennart in the eye and promised their support. Never mind the defectors, he'd still win by at least 10 votes. One by one, delegates cast their votes, Albania first, then Algeria and all the way to voter number 191, Zimbabwe's Leo Mugabe, nephew of his president.

But surely there'd only be 190 votes. One country wasn't voting. Had anyone noticed Kyss's eloquent gesture of defiance? Had anyone asked, why Haiti's empty seat? No-one had and here's why.

Jack Warner had put someone in Kyss's seat. Not a woman, this time. Too risky. A woman is a rarity in football's parliament, the place was swarming with reporters who might notice. No, it had to be a man. A black man who could be relied upon to keep his mouth shut. Warner knew just the fellow.

It was Neville Ferguson, a friend of Warner's since they'd trained together at Mausica teacher's college in Trinidad back in the sixties. Neville was a fan. When interviewed about his famous friend, Neville said that Jack 'liked to have a good time with the ladies and I was amazed he could find the energy to go to church every Sunday morning. He knew that there was a Force far stronger than he was capable of controlling that was running his life.'

And Neville was on the payroll. Jack had made Neville deputy general secretary of the Caribbean Football Union, a job involving lots of international jaunts at football's expense. And Neville had Jack to thank for the fees he earned as an international match commissioner. He'd come to Paris as one of Jack's personal assistants. Suddenly he found himself promoted to delegate with proper plastic accreditation around his neck. Not quite proper, Neville was just a pretend delegate and he wasn't even a citizen of Haiti.

So, sitting in Kyss's seat was Neville Ferguson. Did anyone speak up about the difference? Not Guyana's Colin Klass, who'd failed to spot Vincy Jalal last time. Certainly not Jamaica's Captain Horace Burrell, General Secretary Horace Reid, and almost within touching distance many of the Caribbean Football Union's 30 national associations and several dozen officials. Perhaps FIFA should get a group booking for an eye test.

And while they're at it, perhaps they should have their hearing checked too, because at the roll-call Haiti's man didn't speak French, but said in unmistakeable Caribbean English, 'present'. When Neville cast 'his' vote – you can see him do it on the official FIFA video – a scrutineer looked sharply at him, looked again, but the moment of doubt passed. And Neville's vote was counted along with all the others.

Johansson was stunned. He hadn't won the first round. He'd lost it badly. Blatter had got 111 votes to his 80, not quite enough for a two-thirds victory so they began the second round. But Johansson knew he'd lost it. All that campaigning, all that self-restraint, all that trying to pretend it was a contest between gentlemen, a football family matter. All that trust shattered. He stopped the ballot and, with tears in his eyes, lifted Blatter's hand.

Later, he said with heavy emphasis, 'I was astonished that people I talked to told me they would vote for me and then a lot of them didn't. I've learned a lesson.'

Corinne Blatter spoke the truth when she gushed, 'The vote was won in Africa.' Jack Warner crowed, 'We played a pivotal role in Blatter's victory and we shall be benefiting in both financial and technical areas very shortly.'

At Blatter's victory press conference a German reporter, Jens Weinreich, asked him about allegations that his campaign had been funded from the Gulf. He replied, 'The match is over. The players have already gone to the dressing room, I will not respond.'

It was alleged that US$50,000 bundles had been handed out to African delegates in the Meridien Hotel, supposedly advance payments for development projects in their countries but perhaps unsurprisingly seeming to others like inducements. People talked about bags of cash arriving from the Gulf. In response a Blatter spokesman said, 'Mr Blatter vehemently refutes the allegations and will investigate the source of such malicious reports ... He stresses he reserves the right to take legal action against the seekers to defame him.'

Graham Kelly, chief executive of the English FA, said after Blatter's victory, 'We are delighted he has won, he was the best man for the job.' England's World Cup campaign leader Alec McGivan said, 'If I was German I would be very worried. In the last year their campaign has been ineffective.' Actually, it was the English who should have been worrying, because a week later Blatter said the 2006 tournament should go to Africa and two years later, it went to Germany.

I told Lennart Johansson in April 2002 about the theft of Haiti's vote. He was shocked. He wrote to Blatter, 'I find this revelation very disturbing and must ask you to investigate this urgently.' Blatter did nothing.

I asked CONCACAF Secretary Chuck Blazer about this matter. He responded with a one-line email: 'I am not familiar with the allegations you are making.' I asked CONCACAF vice-president Alan Rothenberg, who'd been sitting towards the back of the hall with his US Soccer delegation. He told me, 'I have no interest in talking to a biased hatchet-man. If you had a shred of impartiality you would recognise the incredible contribution made to the enormous growth of soccer on and off the field by Sepp Blatter, Jack Warner and Chuck Blazer.'

I rang Neville Ferguson. He didn't want to elaborate on the day he became a delegate for a foreign country at the Salle Equinoxe. He hung up and switched on his answering machine.

I tried Jack Warner. He referred my questions to Karen Piper of Trinidad, one of his many lawyers. She told me to stop 'harassing' him or she would take 'appropriate action'. I asked Blatter and his Zurich press minders. They didn't reply to my questions but accidentally copied to me an email Blatter sent to his Caribbean ally: 'Dear Jack, this is part of a never-ending story until we both will be re-elected. Good luck and especially patience. Sepp.'

I flew to Miami in late April 2002 to attend Warner's regional congress, hoping to ask some questions at his press conference. I bumped into him in the lobby of the delightful art deco Loews hotel on South Beach. I said Hello, held out my hand. He declined to shake hands and said, emphatically, in his familiar squeaky lisp, 'You smell!' He was so taken with his own eloquence that he's said it again each time we've met.

Strolling towards the press conference in Loews, I was surprised to find my way blocked by a gentleman much bigger than me. 'Would you be Mr Andrew Jennings?' he asked. 'Yes,' I said, 'Why do you want to know?'

'Mr Blazer says you are not permitted to attend the press conference. You can't go in.' I looked at the accreditation hung around his neck and said, 'So you are Mr Melvin Brennan from Jack and Chuck's New York office. You're an American citizen and you're against freedom of speech?' Melvin, broad as a barn door and nearly as high, looked a bit embarrassed. Still, he wouldn't let me in.

So, Jack didn't like my fragrance and Chuck didn't like my attitude. I felt a bit crest-fallen. I wouldn't be in there to ask Warner about his vote-rigging. I had to make do with reading Warner's unchallenged claim that ran on the news wires later. 'The delegates did not see what all the hullabaloo was about. There is no Haitian problem. The delegate who did not vote gave permission for his vote to be mandated.'

Four years later when I told Kyss what happened to his vote, he was stunned. 'This is the first I've heard of this. I was never sent any information about what happened in Paris. I feel bad about it.' And he looked really sick.

PRESIDENT BLATTER AND THE GOLDEN GOOSE

Leafing through Sepp's expenses

Sunny Hill, 9 June 1998.
Bringg
Bringg
Hello, FIFA House? Oh yes, Good morning Mr Blatter.
I'm sorry, forgive me, yes I saw the news on the TV last night.
Congratulations and Good Morning President Blatter. How is the weather in Paris?
You wish the sign saying President to be moved immediately so it points to your office? Certainly.
And, I beg your pardon Sir, did you say scrap the headed notepaper. What, all of it? Of course. Immediately.
New notepaper to be headed, 'President Joseph S. Blatter.' Right away.
And a sheaf of blank expenses forms to be put on your desk. Yes, Sir. Will that be all? Hello?

FOUL!

Sunny Hill, 13 July 1998. The new president turned his gaze back from the distant Alps, shimmering in the summer heat, to the pile of receipts, bills and invoices littering his desk. Campaigning to become FIFA president was an expensive business, especially when you had to work from home and weren't supposed to use the office facilities. Now, what have we got here? DHL couriers.

Yes, there were some very valuable packages to be moved around the world. Faxing. Yes. And the cell phone. That took a hammering, and look at what they charge. Outrageous. He wrote on the claim form, 'Campagne Présidentielle: Natel, fax, DHL. Nearly thirteen thousand francs; 12,527.70, to be precise.

Then, the travel expenses. It would take forever to itemise them. Better to write down the total and bang it in. 'Frais de voyage Campagne Présidentielle.' 56,032 francs.

Johansson would have a fit if he saw this. But he would never see them. Blatter's expenses were none of his business. In fact they were nobody's business. He didn't have to run them by anybody.

Every member of FIFA's leadership has a private account locked away in the finance department. Their travel expenses, hospitality bills, sometimes private spending on themselves, World Cup ticket purchases, it can all end up in their secret numbered account. Sepp Blatter's isn't quite as secret as it might be. The records show that it was his Golden Goose.

The pages covering the period from December 1997 when Blatter was general secretary, through to December 1999, when he had been president for 18 months, make for curious reading. One day, Blatter puts in a bill for champagne, the next day he's shopping at the Co-op, then he's picking up trainers from Adidas (with FIFA discount) and paying for his personal laundry. The Golden Goose lays eggs, sometimes golden and bejewelled – timepieces from Cartier and Longines. The Golden Goose lays a clutch of tickets for an England v Poland game. In Seoul she lays a weighty load of clothing – handmade suits, most likely, and a big, big, here it comes . . . generous purchase from 'Jeweller to the Stars' Harry Winston of Geneva.

The Golden Goose clucked around Sepp's family and friends as well. When Sepp's brother stayed at the Dolder Grand Hotel, who picked up the tab? Sepp's Golden Goose. When Blatter's daughter, Corinne, went off to live in Chuck Blazer's luxury apartment in Trump Tower on Fifth Avenue, back came the bills from the Precision Limousine company of New York to Dad's Golden Goose. To remind her of home, the Goose laid a subscription to the family's local paper, the *Walliser Bote,* and more shoes from Adidas. It was like a fairy tale. All thanks to Daddy's access to FIFA's bottomless purse.

Sepp's girlfriends, asked how they travelled, could chorus 'I fly FIFA!' The Golden Goose laid eggs for them and showed a talent for tact and logistics. She laid air-tickets so they could spend time with him around the world, and the flights were specially scheduled to avoid unfortunate meetings between rival girlfriends en route.

But the Golden Goose sometimes needs to be fed, even by the man who believes himself the most important in world football. President Blatter had made occasional repayments to FIFA for some personal items but by 30 December 1999 he still hadn't paid back all he should have done. The accountancy firm KPMG was taking over the audit of FIFA's books. On the president's desk was a request from the finance department for 44, 751.95 francs. He took out his chequebook and filled in the numbers on a cheque drawn on his personal account and handed it to accounts clerk Guy-Philippe Mathieu.

Before he sent it off to the bank, Guy-Philippe did a curious thing. He photocopied the cheque on to a sheet of A4 paper, then he scribbled a calculation beneath the image. He rounded Blatter's repayment down to a more manageable 44,000 francs and converted it into US dollars: $27,500 of them.

Then Guy-Philippe did a second calculation; he divided the $27,500 by $500 – the amount President Blatter is entitled to claim for every day he spends outside Switzerland on FIFA business and wrote the answer in German, '55 tags' – 55 days. To emphasise the importance of these 55 days he drew thick penstrokes above and below. So the 44,751.95 francs that Blatter *owed* FIFA had apparently been recast as the number of days he would have to *claim* in expenses in order to be square!

I wrote to Guy-Philippe asking why he did this curious thing and wrote '55 days' on a photocopy of Blatter's cheque. He didn't reply. But in a statement to a Zurich investigating magistrate looking into these transactions and documents in July 2002 Guy-Philippe confirmed that he had written the calculation, adding, 'There was never any cash payment made or any advance of the amount.'

I put the same question to Blatter. He did reply, briefly. 'The handwritten note has nothing to do with this repayment and is of no relevance,' he wrote to me. Blatter insisted that over the next two years after receiving this statement, he repaid to FIFA the money he owed it. Following the conclusion of the Zurich magistrate's investigation, he claimed, 'All the allegations that had been made were dismissed.'

SEPP PATTED his pocket, retrieved the precious envelope that he'd been guarding since his last, taut, meeting with Havelange in Paris and picked up his phone. 'Yes, Sepp?' breathed Helen in the next room. 'Send up Erwin,' said the boss.

The Finance Director's heart must have beaten a little faster as he walked around the corridor to what he, like the others, must now learn to call the President's Office. This was their first formal meeting since Paris. Did he still have the boss's confidence? Was the man he called his best friend, JSB, still his friend? What did he want? Helen hadn't said. Erwin knocked. 'Enter.' 'Sepp?' Blatter welcomed Erwin warmly. It wasn't the sack, today.

He presented Erwin with a most important envelope. Erwin went back to his office, closed the door on Guy-Philippe and the secretaries and opened the envelope. It was a memo from the office of Joao Havelange – the very last memo he'd written before leaving the presidency. Above Havelange's signature was an instruction to pay Joseph S. Blatter a six-figure loyalty bonus, a *prime de fidelité*, every 1 July. For good measure, it was back-dated to July 1997. So, Sepp was in for two year's bonus. And a very handsome windfall every July for the rest of his years at the top. Erwin placed Havelange's order in the red, confidential salaries file to which he alone had access.

THEY WERE the troika that knew everything and disclosed the minimum about FIFA's finances. Sepp Blatter, Julio Grondona and Erwin Schmid. Grondona had the self-confidence of a man who had survived more than two decades presiding over football in Argentina. Havelange knew him well from their years in Latin America and put him in charge of FIFA's finance committee in 1996.

Grondona was now Blatter's senior vice-president and the second most important man in world football, but he had a knack of making his big, rounded frame seem insignificant. At the occasional press conference they shared, all eyes would turn to the articulate, gesticulating Blatter. Grondona, sitting silent to one side, listening to translation of the reporters' questions through his headphones, would slowly slump, eyes hooded, looking down at the desk, not seeking contact.

Grondona had done all he could to help get Blatter elected. Now, in this new era, FIFA awash with cash, it was time for Blatter to improve the rewards for the people at the top. He began with a handsome salary of US$50,000 a year for all 23 volunteer members of the executive committee, FIFA's cabinet. Announcing this to the press in September 1998 the President thanked Grondona, cooing, 'The Finance Committee has been very gracious and generous.'

That wasn't the full story. There was more they didn't announce.

Sepp and Grondona instructed FIFA's advisors to negotiate a favourable tax deal with the Swiss authorities and in March 2000 the advisors wrote to say they had got one. Because the cabinet members were foreigners the Zurich cantonal authorities would settle for a 10 per cent deduction instead of the usual 25 per cent for residents.

Better still, FIFA paid the tax for them, so every six months each member receives a cheque for US$25,000 and a note to show their local tax inspector that tax has been paid.

When committee members go on the road all their expenses are met, as you'd expect. Taxis, trains and planes, hotels and restaurants are all paid for by FIFA. These men tend to have expensive tastes – a hotel with less than five stars is hardly a hotel – and for everything, FIFA foots the bill.

On top of all that, each member is encouraged to claim an extra 'allowance' of US$500 a day whenever he travels on FIFA business. As there are few one-day trips, the allowances soon mount up.

The flow of cash into other people's pockets grew as Blatter created more committees. He now has in his gift more than 300 committee positions, all distributing expenses and allowances. His nominees have to go before the executive committee for approval and the sound of rubber stamps echoes through the Alps.

Just as the president has his Golden Goose, so every member of the executive committee can have a Silver Goose, an expense account where he can accumulate the various payments. According to records I have seen, at least one member stashes tens of thousands of dollars in Zurich. From time to time the money is withdrawn in cash and shipped home. When the drug police began to crack down on travellers carrying more than US$10,000 in cash at least one member began sending girlfriends to Switzerland at FIFA's expense to suitcase a share of the money home.

Sunny Hill, 18 December 2000. 'My apologies for disturbing you for the third time on this matter,' wrote accounts clerk Guy-Philippe Mathieu despairingly to general secretary, Michel Zen-Ruffinen. To emphasise his concern, his desire to be relieved of an unpleasant burden, he copied it to FIFA's new finance chief, Urs Linsi. Among Guy-Philippe's tasks was the unenviable chore of processing expense claims submitted by his employers, the executive committee.

Uniquely, FIFA's top dogs have given themselves permission to submit expense claims without attaching any evidence that they actually spent the money. They don't have to bother collecting receipts, hotel and restaurant bills, taxi chits, credit card slips, airline invoices. They can, if they wish, bang in a demand for any amount of money they think they can get away with.

Honest members scrupulously document every claim they make. Others don't and Guy-Philippe has to make judgements. On this occasion he had had enough. One member had recently pocketed US$44,000 for his involvement in a modest FIFA tournament. Now the same man wanted US$27,420 in 'settlement of his mission last week in Acapulco'.

That wasn't all. He wanted a further US$13,717 for a trip from his home to Zurich. He'd transited through London, stayed two nights in a hotel at a cost of US$700, and getting around town had cost another US$150. He did not produce a scrap of paper to justify his demands.

In his grey-walled office overlooking the car park Guy-Philippe, the mildest of men, blew his top. He scribbled on the claim, 'Last year he defrauded us.' If that wasn't clear enough Guy-Philippe added, 'Ripped off.'

I WANTED to give Blatter a chance to tell his side of the story. I sent him detailed questions about how FIFA's money was spent. It didn't take him long to work out I'd been leaked a copy of his expense account. He banned me from his press conferences. Why did he ban me? Was it a punishment? Was he worried that I might, in front of the world's press, start waving documents that might shed some light on the truth?

Sadly I couldn't ask him to his face about the Golden Goose and the eggs it laid for him. A colleague did me a favour, went along to a press conference in April 2003 and asked him if he had charged any of his presidential campaign expenses to FIFA. 'Absolute nonsense,' he insisted. After the vehement denials in 1998, he couldn't really say anything else.

Another colleague emailed Blatter's new spokesman, the youthful Markus Siegler, asking him to explain why Blatter put in the claim for nearly 70,000 francs he'd spent on travel couriers, faxes and cell-phones during his presidential campaign.

'It is clear to us that in the course of your self-appointed status as watchdog over the wellbeing of FIFA, you are running out of material of any relevance whatsoever,' replied Markus, 'and therefore resort to ever more meaningless bits of "information" obtained unlawfully, be it by theft committed by third parties or other means that shed an even more dubious light on some of your sources and/or contributors.'

Markus raged on, 'But feel free to publish yet another lie, yet another fabrication which we shall simply add to the list of charges that are presently being prepared.' It was all rather illogical. I didn't like to explain to Markus; he's bright enough to see it for himself. If these bits of information were indeed the real thing, however they'd been obtained, then they were the basis, not of a lie, but of the simple truth.

I think Markus must have regretted his crossness because when I emailed him asking why members don't have to produce receipts when they claim their expenses, he was all sweetness though not a lot of light. 'As a matter of principle lack of documentation is not fatal to a proper claim for expenses,' he told me, 'provided proper procedures are followed which is FIFA's practice.' But how can you have a 'proper procedure' without receipts?

I asked Markus, 'Is it true there are problems with claims from other members?' He said, 'That question is impertinent.'

IN MAY 2000, before they set off for the Olympics in Sydney there was sad news for FIFA's cabinet members. General Secretary Michel Zen-Ruffinen sent them a memo, saying, 'We shall try to accommodate you in keeping with our standards but the number of junior suites has been restricted to an absolute minimum and cannot be guaranteed.'

The news got worse. 'Unfortunately it will not be possible to give you personally assigned cars.' To make up for the disappointment President Blatter authorised a new category of expenses that didn't have to be documented or accounted for. 'As regards the person (wife/partner) accompanying you, we are pleased to inform you that she will receive a daily allowance of US$200 – and the travel costs reimbursed.' This was on top of the US$500 a day the member was charging for attending the Olympics, all expenses paid.

'MR PRESIDENT, HOW MUCH DOES FIFA PAY YOU?'

'Er . . .'

IN THE CORPORATE world it is standard practice for company reports to include details of directors' salaries, perks and pension packages. It's a matter of transparency, so shareholders can see what these people are doing with their money.

What happens when you ask FIFA about the rewards paid to its administrators? Can stakeholders and fans find out what slice of the billions of dollars generated by the World Cup is pocketed by its senior officials? What does Sepp Blatter earn?

Urs Linsi, Blatter's finance director is the man to ask. And he trumpets his commitment to transparency. In January 2003 he granted a no-holds-barred, ask-me-anything-you-damn-well-like exclusive interview to . . . a press officer he employs at fifa.com. It was headlined, 'We have to be as transparent as possible.'

He insisted that 'FIFA is a healthy, clean and transparent organisation with nothing to hide.' Then, in more reflective mood

Mr Linsi noted, 'We should always remember to let the media and the public know what we are doing. There is huge public interest in FIFA, therefore we have to be as transparent as possible. We will try to communicate in a more open way concerning football matters so the world can believe us and be proud of their federation.'

I emailed Urs Linsi and asked him if he would tell me what the president earns in salary, pension contributions, cars, bonuses and any other perks.

He didn't reply.

Instead, FIFA spokesman Markus Siegler wrote to me: 'Dear Mr Jennings, We can answer your question as follows: The matter of the compensation (not salary!) of the President for this term was dealt with and decided unanimously at the Finance Committee (in the presence of all members) at its meeting on 15 December 2002 in Madrid. The respective minutes have been ratified by the Executive Committee at its last meeting on 6/7 March 2003 here in Zurich. Thanks for your understanding.'

I emailed back to Siegler. Actually, no, I didn't understand.

Why were he and Linsi refusing to reveal even one fact, one sum of money, not even the tiniest clue about Blatter's rewards package? 'We must abide by internal rules and cultural traditions,' Siegler explained. 'In Switzerland, salaries or income are simply not published. Also, you must not question FIFA's dedication to transparency.'

Markus, a former journalist asked me, a journalist, 'Who would like to know Mr Blatter's salary, as a matter of interest?'

Well, the public, Mr Siegler. Remember them?

Vice-President Chung Mong-Joon from Korea tried to find out in 2002. He wrote to Jack Warner and pointed out that when vice-president Lennart Johansson asked how much Blatter trousered he was told, 'The remuneration of the President was fixed by the finance committee at the same time as the indemnity to the executive committee was ratified.'

Mr Chung noted, 'This is an example of the arrogance of the FIFA President. Why do you think I cannot get a straight answer for this legitimate question?' Chung asked Warner, how much is Blatter paid?

Warner replied to Chung, his fellow committee member, 'Dear MJ, I vacillated for some time on whether I should dignify your letter to me with a reply or not. And then, today, I decided to reply to you if only because I did not want to leave you with the false impression that your perfidious letter is worth the paper on which it has been written.'

He concluded, 'I judge myself by such universal virtues as honesty, integrity, loyalty and friendship.'

Blatter's salary remains a secret. Inside FIFA they say 4 million francs (about £1.7 million) sounds about right. And his secret employment contract is said to contain a poison pill. Sack Blatter and FIFA must pay him 24 million francs. That's nearly £11 million. The allowance paid towards the cost of his roof-top apartment in Zollikon is said to cost FIFA 8,000 francs a month (almost £1,000 a week), then there's the top-of-the-line Mercedes.

And the pension? Another secret matter. On top of all that, the bonuses. But how many? He always received a bonus from his earliest days as general secretary. Was Havelange's farewell, back-dated present a second one? Could there be any more, extracted from any of his other responsibilities at FIFA?

Whatever Blatter's friends on the finance committee pay him, it's not enough. It can't be, because Blatter still needs to claim that US$500 a day pocket money.

Whenever he's in your country, or making a speech or receiving an award anywhere outside Switzerland, he's pocketing US$500 a day, as Guy-Philippe Mathieu acknowledged when processing Blatter's expenses repayment. He usually spends at least 150 days on the road and that's worth US$75,000. In his busier years he can hope to claim as much as US$125,000 on top of his salary and other perks – just for going to work, first class with red carpets waiting at the airport.

The Honorary President, a title Havelange accepted from his last congress in Paris in 1998, gets a pension but FIFA won't say how much. They won't say anything about what the Brazilian has trousered in the past and continues to take. It is believed that from 1994 he was paid US$125,000 annually. He travels extensively and expensively on what FIFA calls 'representational duties' and can charge for a companion. His driver shows up with a Mercedes when required, anywhere in the world from Bamako to Salt Lake City. Havelange retains his FIFA credit card.

SEPP BLATTER has lived in Zurich since 1975, but registered his tax affairs on the other side of the country in Valais, the canton where he grew up and which has lower rates.

Then he discovered the tax-avoider's paradise. Eighty kilometres east of Zurich is the tiny canton of Appenzell, only 15,000 people living in six villages. A rural community with not much to raise taxes on, the canton had gone into the business of doing tax deals with wealthy people. The local politicians reckoned that some money was better than none at all and if other cantons lost out, too bad. They advertise that their canton is a product and the tax office is a sales office and welcome people to come and negotiate their own secret deal. They say to rich Swiss and foreigners, 'You will never walk alone, you will always find friends who are on your side and support you.'

The burghers of Appenzell are notorious in secretive Switzerland for their dislike of transparency in public affairs. Their local dialect word, *heimlichfeiss*, that translates roughly as 'clandestine', sums up their opposition to openness. Blatter registered his tax affairs in Appenzell and told the Zurich authorities that he was a *Wochenaufenthalter* – he lived in Zurich only during the week.

Life was sweet. Then in the autumn of 1995 the Swiss tabloid *Blick* came knocking at Blatter's Zurich address with some questions. Could he tell them the address where he was registered in Appenzell? Blatter tried and got it wrong. Then he tried again and still got it wrong. Eventually the *Blick* reporters had to tell him. They estimated that Blatter was saving at least 250,000 Swiss francs (£110,000) a year on his tax bill and in time-honoured tabloid style, they delivered their dossier to the Zurich Canton tax inspectors.

Blatter volunteered his version of the story to a local paper from his home canton of Valais, the *Walliser Bote*. First, he asked his old friends and neighbours to believe him – there was no story. A successful man like himself was always going to be a target for the jealous and the sensationalist press. It was nothing more than the prejudice of city slickers in Zurich looking down their noses at a country boy who had done well for himself. It might also be the case that he was being targeted in what was really a clandestine attack on Havelange.

Talk of an investigation by the Zurich authorities into his tax affairs was incorrect, he said. There was some checking going on but merely a clarification of his address. He said he couldn't reveal any more information because he had transferred his tax registration to Appenzell for very private reasons to do with his emotional life.

What Blatter didn't tell the reporters from Valais or from *Blick* or indeed anybody else outside FIFA's finance office is that he doesn't pay tax on his earnings. FIFA pays it for him.

IN THE LATE Spring of 2000, the Zurich tax inspectors gave FIFA a month's warning that they were coming to conduct an audit of their tax files. The KPMG team that took over the auditing of FIFA's books in 2000 was led by Fredy Luthiger, a partner from their Zurich office. Fredy, long, slim, bespectacled, occasionally running his delicate fingers through his white hair, seems like a man who's never happier than when he's spending his days reading spreadsheets.

When challenged about some of the far from transparent financial procedures at FIFA, the president, his mouthpieces and his lawyers can bellow from the same hymn sheet, 'It's been audited by KPMG!' and claim that gives them an absolute justification to refuse to answer more questions.

I wrote to Fredy asking him why members can claim expenses without receipts. Fredy replied that his professional code of ethics prevents him discussing his client's business. One specific thing Fredy couldn't talk about was the confidential Management Letter he submitted to FIFA in 2000 and the warning he gave, that FIFA had not been obeying its duties under taxation processes.

Fredy clearly spelled out his message. 'There exists a risk of being held accountable because of non-compliance.' If Fredy had used the language of the street criminal he might have warned, 'If you don't get this sorted fast, guv, you'll be nicked.'

In his Management Letter for 2001 that he submitted to FIFA the following year, Fredy had to point to more embarrassing problems. He had been examining the individual accounts that every one of the 200 or so national associations and the six regional confederations has with FIFA. They list payments, debts, loans, development funds and secret purchases of huge quantities of World Cup tickets. What a mess they were.

During Blatter's years as general secretary FIFA hadn't always chased up debts. Seventy-five per cent of the accounts – that's around 150 of the 200 associations – had lingering debts.

Why hadn't FIFA made the associations pay their debts? They're not saying. Fredy said that this 'was not satisfactory'. Then he talked as tough as most accountants who have just picked up a big, prestigious piece of business. 'We recommend taking action against such associations.'

FROM CARROTS AND STICKS ...

Blatter builds his citadel

LIFE CAN BE TOUGH for powerful men. Sometimes they have to sacrifice their friends on the altar of their ambition. As new president, Sepp Blatter regarded with fresh eyes his friend Michel Zen-Ruffinen. For years as general secretary Sepp had been proud to call his deputy 'my protégé'. They both grew up in the canton of Valais in the south. Blatter studied in Lausanne, Zen-Ruffinen graduated in law from the university in Geneva, further along the lakeside.

Blatter hired Zen-Ruffinen in 1986 to take charge of refereeing and work in FIFA's legal department. Tall, dark, lean and handsome he was the youngest referee to control first division games in Switzerland and in 1993 he passed his exams and qualified to be an international class referee. He gave up the hobby in 1995 when Blatter made him deputy general secretary. And when Sepp was forced to stand down to campaign for the presidency, Michel stepped into his shoes. Now, aged 39, Zen-Ruffinen was poised to receive his mentor's blessing and become the new general secretary.

But Blatter knew how dangerous general secretaries could be. Hadn't he tried to oust Havelange? A strong general secretary might be death to Blatter's ambition. He had lived a long time in sports politics and he had learned how to survive. Just look at that marvellous survivor, Juan Antonio Samaranch. He'd dismissed his director general, made himself executive president and micro-managed every aspect of the organisation.

Primo Nebiolo, another Dassler placeman, had done the same at track and field. They were survivors, they took control, and Sepp Blatter was going to take control, he was going to make the world's most popular game dance to his tune.

Blatter set in motion his plan to take total control of FIFA. Some of the employees up on Sunny Hill thought they knew why. It wasn't just about money, the secret tax-paid remuneration and perks-package. Some said his firm hold on FIFA and its international empire gave him the security he lacked in a life littered with the wreckage of failed marriages and countless meaningless relationships.

So Blatter moved to have Michel Zen-Ruffinen sidelined. There was another Michel in Sepp's life. France's Michel Platini, three times a World Cup hero. He hadn't lost his good looks and his charisma could light up a room. A fabulous goal-scorer, three times European Footballer of the Year, and World Footballer of the Year in 1985, Platini had gone from French team manager to chair the organising committee for the 1998 World Cup in France. He too had ambitions to rise up FIFA.

Blatter's plan was to reconstruct FIFA so that he was Executive President. In his office at 7am each day he'd receive reports from his top two lieutenants. Michel Platini would take charge of football affairs – 'my sporting conscience' Blatter was already calling him – and Michel Zen-Ruffinen would be head of administration, a paper shuffler, lacking power. Blatter would immerse himself in marketing and money, the areas of his empire where the real power lay.

But FIFA's executive committee, more than half of them still smarting from Blatter's manipulations during his election campaign, were in no mood to create a super-president. Meeting in Zurich on 3 December 1998 they insisted that the office of general secretary must be maintained. Teeth clenched, the president welcomed Zen-Ruffinen's promotion.

But it was still early days in Blatter's reign. It takes time to build citadels. So, Blatter had to accept Zen-Ruffinen as general secretary. So what? He could manoeuvre to rob the man of power. When the executive committee met again on 11 March 1999 around the boardroom table in the new concrete and glass building next to the mansion on Sunny Hill, Blatter gestured warmly to the best-known face at the table, the only face there that said football.

'A warm welcome please to Michel Platini, a household name who really needs no introduction, he will be an advisor to the President and also please meet, I'm sure many of you remember him from last year, Jerome Champagne, in the new post of my personal advisor. His past experience as head of protocol for France '98 and in the French diplomatic corps aptly qualify him for this post.' Did anyone guess that this was the start of Blatter's parallel administration, an outfit that would split FIFA's soul?

Blatter surveyed his executive committee, a mix of men who were in his debt, men who could be bought, good men who had been put firmly in their place or soundly beaten. And men who were biding their time, building their own power bases, who might some day strike Blatter down if they could. Looking around the table it was clear, this wasn't about football, it was about power. Some of these people had been put there by continental federations, they didn't all see things Blatter's way. Not yet, but he could work on it. For now, Blatter had to keep friend and foe, in the room and around the world of football, busy. Fortunately, he had the power to nominate more than 300 lucky officials to seats on committees. They would rack up the kind of expenses and allowances that after a while they'd find hard to live without.

Just a few feet away from the president sat vice-president Lennart Johansson. In the hours after the Paris vote his aides at UEFA had quietly briefed reporters that they would not accept the result. Then it dawned on them that there was nothing they could do, Havelange and Blatter had outwitted them. Johansson, asked if bribes had been paid by Blatter's camp, said stiffly, 'I have no proof of this and I refuse to speculate. I do not want to appear a bad loser and I congratulate Mr Blatter on his success.'

Johansson went back to lick his wounds in European football's headquarters in South Switzerland, presiding over the UEFA Cup and the Champions' League. Johansson was a rare one; he wasn't there for the expense account and some people respected him for that. He was capable, too. So Blatter showed a little respect to Johansson and the European nations he represented, and put him in charge of the committee organising the next World Cup in 2002. That would keep his mind off the African bribery rumours. He'd have to work hard to bring harmony to the tournament in Korea, a country that had spent the first half of the previous century under the boot of the other joint host, Japan. So Johansson was busy, and these days his health wasn't the best and, just in case he should think to stir trouble again, Blatter installed his own man, the loyal Julio Grondona, to be his deputy.

Grondona was more than the senior vice-president, he was chairman of the finance committee, the one that mattered most to Blatter. He also chaired the marketing and television board.

Grondona's deputy at finance was Jack Warner, they took the key money decisions and the minutes of such meetings were never published. Grondona had some distasteful opinions – he didn't think much of Jews – but despite expressing his views on television that didn't harm his career at FIFA.

Jack Warner was a protégé of Havelange. He was a great man to have on your side, a fiercely loyal supporter. His association with FIFA had made him a fortune. It was a matter of prestige to be on the World Cup committee and no vice-president could be left off. He also controlled two of the potentially most lucrative committees in international football, the ones organising youth tournaments.

Jack was the man who could give the thumbs up – or down – to countries vying to host these championships, staged every two years. Sure, they weren't the big ones but some countries, like the oil and gas-rich potentates of the Gulf, who could only dream of hosting the World Cup, badly wanted the youth tournaments.

Warner complained about slights real and imagined, but really his life was good. He once told a Trinidad reporter that he was a multi-millionaire, thanks to world football. 'I began buying properties across Trinidad from the salary and allowances I received from FIFA. I have had one or two good fortunes. I get ultra-fantastic paycheques.' The former schoolteacher loved to flaunt his wealth and show off the solid-gold paper knife given to him by King Fahd of Saudi Arabia.

Jack's side-kick, Chuck Blazer, his general secretary who ran CONCACAF from their New York office, was the only member of the executive committee who wasn't elected by the rank and file. He was Jack's personal appointee. When Jack looked his regional confederation in the eye and told them that Chuck would take the FIFA seat, not one mouse roared.

Chuck was into money as much as Jack was and he kept

a close eye on the stock markets. Like some other Americans who rose to the top of world football, he'd never played the game, only stumbled across it and spotted a lucrative business opportunity.

You could see why Blatter chose Chuck to head the media committee. Chuck knew how to hold a door tight shut against enquiries and he had an astonishing way of giving off hostility without any discernable effort, as if by perspiration alone. And he could switch on the charm when it was needed. Chuck was a favourite in Zurich and so was his talented daughter Marci Blazer, who got a seat on FIFA's legal committee. Few lawyers in the world could claim membership of world football's 'Commission de Questions Juridiques.'

Mohamed Bin Hammam from Qatar looked younger than his mid-50s. He'd sat at this boardroom table for two years and deserved a reward for his fine work during the election campaign that left Johansson in tears. Blatter gave him the top job at the new Goal Bureau. The Bureau had a whacking US$100 million to spend at Bin Hammam's discretion, and that was on top of the US$1 million that each national association would get from the new television money.

Bin Hammam's Goal Bureau would entertain applications from national associations who wanted new offices, pitches and equipment. The president called this 'tailor-made solutions' and he would be travelling the world frenetically in the next three years as the great benefactor.

Sometimes Bin Hammam travelled with Blatter to the ribbon-cutting ceremonies but he made as many trips alone, with his personal entourage, descending from the skies, graciously receiving flowery speeches of gratitude. And who wouldn't defer to a man who can influence an Emir, a ruler endowed with deep deposits of natural gas, one of the richest men in the world?

The man with the money from Qatar was a rising star, popping

up everywhere on the committees that mattered. He helped
Grondona and Warner at the finance committee. He chaired the
technical committee. A seat on the national associations committee gave him more contact with the grassroots, handing out
money. Bin Hammam was gluing together his own band of
officials who felt personal loyalty to him, not yet a parallel empire
but in time he might threaten the president. Bin Hammam had
helped put Blatter up there and in time, Bin Hammam might take
Blatter down.

Blatter rewarded the silver-haired Russian Viacheslav Koloskov
with chair of the national associations committee. In the old
Soviet days he'd kept Eastern Europe solidly in line behind the
Zurich establishment. When that disintegrating bloc lost its vice-
presidency Koloskov found himself out in the cold. As Blatter
came in as president, Koloskov had the bad luck to leave the
executive committee at the very moment when members were
awarded a tax-free US$50,000 dollars a year.

Never mind, Blatter paid him US$100,000 anyway. When this
payment came to light in 2002, Blatter said maybe he should
have told the Finance Committee about it, but he also emphasised
that Koloskov had been doing wonderful work for football
in Eastern Europe. 'There was no corruption on my part,' said
Blatter. 'To claim so is tantamount to slander.'

Havelange wasn't actually in Sepp's boardroom, but he might
as well have been. His nominee was there. Son-in-law Ricardo
Teixeira, whose wheeling and dealing in Brazil had hit the headlines, represented the minority sulking tendency. Havelange had
never wanted to go and his Brazilian entourage resented their
loss of power over FIFA's money. Ricardo harboured dreams
that if his national team went on winning the World Cup he
could bid to oust Blatter. He was one of the babies at the table,
born in 1947 – eleven years younger than the new president, two

years younger than Bin Hammam. Ricardo had time on his side.

Blatter needed to keep Ricardo busy in a job that had no influence. Step forward Ricardo Teixeira, chair of the Futsal committee, master of indoor soccer. Blatter cast about for another position short on political power and influence and made him deputy chair of the referees' committee in late 1999. It was an unlikely job for a man facing allegations of corruption at home in Brazil.

Further round the table, David Will, the Scottish vice-president nominated by the four British associations, wasn't going to lead any revolutions but he could be sticky on points of principle. So Blatter gave him FIFA's legal committee to run and issue tickets for the World Cup. That's almost two full-time jobs. Something always goes wrong with the tickets and inevitably he'd be deluged with noisy complaints just as the president's re-election campaign peaked in the weeks before a World Cup tournament.

The biggest potential threat for now was the Korean, Chung Mong-Joon. He was probably the richest man in the room, a member of the Hyundai family. A vice-president from Asia, he took a dim view of the shabbiness at FIFA and would come into greater prominence as the 2002 World Cup was held in his country. He spoke English and German, was a Trustee at Johns Hopkins University in Baltimore and a FIFA youngster – born as recently as 1951. If he didn't decide to run for the presidency of Korea he might go after FIFA's top job. From Blatter's viewpoint, Chung was dangerous: very bright and, with his boyish smile, worryingly good looking.

Fortunately he was kept busy in Seoul and he accepted Blatter's offer to chair the almost invisible protocol committee. The other threat in sight was Issa Hayatou from Cameroon, a FIFA vice-president and president of the African confederation. Hayatou and his large continent had to be shown some respect. So Blatter gave him a couple of committees – Olympic football, a lot of hard work, and the Confederations Cup tournament which sounds important and costs a lot, but nobody takes it seriously.

It was hard work filling the hundreds of positions on FIFA's ever-growing list of committees, weighing up who had a powerful backer, who'd like the allowances and expenses, who would pledge their vote for a seat. Then there was the delicacy needed for appointments to the Football Committee where living legends like Franz Beckenbauer, Sir Bobby Charlton, Pelé, Eusebio and George Weah came up with suggestions about the future of the game that were widely reported and then, more often than not, sidelined. The legends were useful props to put beside a smiling Sepp in happy snaps that were swiftly posted on fifa.com.

And what were all these important men, gathered at vast expense, here to do? Were there vital decisions to be made for the good of football? Not really, the decisions that mattered were made in private among Blatter's inner clique.

On Blatter's executive committee table were piles of reports, reports on the Confederations Cup and the World Youth Championship. They all lost money but gave less powerful soccer nations opportunities to compete internationally and more administrators a chance to share in Sepp Blatter's largesse.

The executive committee listened politely while Blatter prepared to offer an apology. A while back Blatter, dreaming aloud, had blurted out to a news reporter that he was thinking of holding the World Cup every two years.

The football press were outraged. It would wreck the world game. Football's finest players would be permanently tied up in round after round of qualifying games. It would be death to the leagues. Clubs and fans would hardly ever see their stars, always absent travelling, training, playing and picking up injuries with their national squads.

Fans in Europe's top leagues would have to make do with watching reserve teams doing their best. If you wanted to destroy football, this would be a brilliant strategy. But there was one good thing in it. A World Cup every two years would mean double the money: twice the television fees, twice as much from McDonald's and Coca-Cola.

Members of the executive were furious. A change so momentous should be discussed first by them before a whiff of it reached the press. Blatter told the members: 'I feel I owe you an explanation. I unwittingly mentioned the idea of a World Cup every two years at a press interview, never suspecting that it would be construed as revolutionary and unleash a storm of emotion. It was only when some members had expressed annoyance at finding this out through the media that I realised I should have informed them before allowing my enthusiasm to run away with me. I therefore ask you to accept my apologies and in future I will avoid such a situation arising. Thank you.'

It was the same patter that powerful men everywhere, prime ministers, presidents, corporate chiefs, tend to offer, when they forget for a moment that they owe a duty to some kind of democratic process and start making up policy on the hoof. And it was just as sincerely meant.

14

DIVIDE AND RULE

FIFA's civil war

IT DIDN'T take long for the FIFA workforce to figure out that Jerome Champagne was something more than an advisor to Blatter. Michel Zen-Ruffinen might have had the general secretary's title but big, brooding Jerome had got the job. He'd got the flash new Mercedes too, and 23,000 Swiss francs (£10,000) a month, the highest salary in the building after Blatter, and an apartment high up near the Sunny Hill mansion. His hiring had been handled with the utmost discretion and when he'd arrived in January 1999, he preferred a low profile, describing his new job as 'A little like a principal private secretary, I organise the calendar, the communications and the travels of the president.'

Jerome's description of himself suggested the kind of modesty you'd expect of a man schooled in diplomacy's black arts. Two decades earlier he'd spent too many of his student days freelancing at a French football magazine, neglected his studies and failed to complete his course at the National School of Administration which admits only the brightest of the bright, but that didn't hold him back. Champagne studied Oriental languages – he speaks English, Spanish, German, Portuguese, Chinese and Arabic – then political science, before joining France's ministry of foreign affairs and, aged 25, was posted as a cultural attaché to Oman. After a spell in Cuba he moved to Los Angeles where he was appointed consul-general and met his American wife.

In July 1994, three days before the Brazil–Italy World Cup Final at the Los Angeles Rose Bowl, consul-general Champagne staged a garden party in Beverley Hills for members of the France '98 Organising Committee. Three years later Champagne was number two in the embassy in Brasilia, renewing an acquaintanceship with Michel Platini who was President Jacques Chirac's sidekick on a goodwill tour of Latin America. By 1998 the French government bought Jerome home and put him in charge of state protocol at the World Cup, where he struck up a relationship with Sepp Blatter.

Blatter saw a man he could use, a collaborator, a bodyguard, a campaign manager for the next FIFA presidential elections in three years time but not a man equipped to replace him. A perfect shadow general secretary. And a brilliant advance man with a turn of phrase that made his boss look good. 'We live in an individualistic and uneven world in which the short term becomes the rule,' Jerome told *France Football*. 'It is necessary to restore values like solidarity and universality. I would not be where I am today if I did not share these ideals with Joseph Blatter.'

After FIFA's executive committee blocked Blatter's re-organisation plans, Michel Platini established his own office in Paris with his secretary Odile Lanceau and press officer Alain Leiblang. Platini's staff were paid nearly 18,000 francs (£8,000) a month, more than most salaries up on Sunny Hill.

As the new, parallel FIFA management team grew, so the

people who thought they were running FIFA found themselves out of favour, and sometimes out of work. Blatter evicted his old friend Erwin Schmid in mid-1999 and out the door went an unrivalled encyclopaedic knowledge of the Blatter years. Erwin knew everything about FIFA's bank records and the expenses and bonuses available to Blatter and Havelange. Erwin took legal action to secure a bigger pay-off and won.

Blatter could now choose the money man he wanted for his new regime and the strong belief up on Sunny Hill was that the recommendation came from a senior executive at marketing agents ISL.

Urs Linsi had just turned 50 and spent most of his working life in the leasing department of the Credit Suisse bank. Immaculately dressed, and with his domed head and cautious manner, Linsi looked like a banker but a tough heart beat beneath the conservative clothes. A world-class triathlete, he started the FIFA endurance race as finance director. His colleagues were impressed by his work rate in his first few months, staying so late at night in the office. 'He obviously found what he was looking for,' said a colleague sourly after Blatter confirmed him in his job.

'He looks like Tom Cruise,' giggled the secretaries when the handsome Flavio Battaini joined as a junior lawyer in 1996. He'd been on Blatter's campaign plane in Africa and his name was on the new appointments roster in January 1999, as Director of Marketing. Flavio had no record in marketing beyond reading contracts in FIFA's legal department. Perhaps appointing Flavio with his limited experience might leave Blatter free to continue his dealings with Jean-Marie Weber without interference.

The president personally hired his new personnel chief, a key figure in FIFA's reorganisation. Michael Schallhart, in his late 30s, was an international ice hockey referee who'd worked for the Samaritans. Blatter recruited his own personal propaganda man, a direct link to the media that would circumnavigate FIFA's communications department run by Englishman Keith Cooper. Blatter chose Markus Siegler, a tall and good-looking former local reporter who had been freelancing for FIFA. His boyish charm and warm smile helped him sell the president's positive messages.

The president's plans to divide and rule were working. FIFA had an administration run in theory by General Secretary Michel Zen-Ruffinen and a parallel and challenging administration led by shadow General Secretary Jerome Champagne. The house was divided. Bitterness and distrust festered. The people who did all the work felt betrayed. Their bosses didn't seem to be in charge any more. Who were they working for? Blatter and his tight little team seemed to be making all the decisions. Sometimes Zen-Ruffinen sat in on the inner-circle's meetings but he wasn't made welcome. They seemed to be snatching power from right under his feet.

Blatter had a name for his new parallel administration, the *Führungscrew*, the 'F-Crew' or 'Leadership Crew'. People on the staff felt it was an insult to Zen-Ruffinen and, by extension, an insult to them. Blatter claimed, 'The F-crew is a consultative body that aims to promote internal communication and accelerate problem solving.'

It was having the opposite effect. Staff morale was in terrible shape. Even Blatter could see that all was not well. He turned to Norwegian Bjorn Johansson, who runs a small but classy head-hunting consultancy for top executives from his top-floor offices by the lakeside in Zurich. Bjorn advised him to try to heal FIFA's wounds.

Bjorn knew a bit about unhappy organisations. He felt that time apart sometimes helped. And so in February 2000 he took FIFA's senior managers – without Sepp or his clique – off up Lake Constance to the health spa of Bad Ragaz, a haven of thermal baths and ski slopes, that promised 'year round caressing for souls and bodies'. After all the acrimony, FIFA people needed some caressing. Bjorn encouraged them to talk and he listened.

The managers begged for improvements in internal communications. They wanted problems to be solved and open, honest and fair discussions. They wanted closer co-operation with the President and wanted to know where FIFA was heading.

They complained that FIFA was in one terrible mess. FIFA's most important job, its reason for being, was staging the football World Cup, and the other competitions for women and youngsters. Yet with just 18 months left before the World Cup, they hadn't even got a director of competitions. And too many of the junior managers didn't know what they're doing. They weren't convinced that decisions were being made for the good of the game, and were concerned that staff in the development department were not being consulted about how the money was spent.

After the counselling sessions had finished for the day, Sepp Blatter turned up from Zurich for the formal dinner, like an errant husband crashing in late on the dysfunctional family therapy session, hoping a big box of fancy chocolates would set everything right. He handed out his brochure *The House of FIFA, Vision and Aspirations*.

Blatter assured them his heart and soul was in football and FIFA, and his vision was to make the game better and take it to the world. Then he told them their priorities were the next congress, the World Cup – and getting him re-elected!

As Blatter's limousine swept away, the team talked freely again. They agreed that the open and honest atmosphere of the meetings changed during the dinner thrown by the President. They felt it had been right to exclude the President from their discussions. You just couldn't speak freely with Blatter around.

*   *   *

EVEN BLATTER could see that his *Führungscrew* plan wasn't working. Setting up a parallel administration had been intended to destabilise general secretary Zen-Ruffinen, not enrage and depress all the senior managers. Blatter pondered on the problem and came up with a solution.

They needed re-educating. He did what autocrats throughout the business world had done before him. He summoned McKinsey, the management consultants. By sheer coincidence, McKinsey's head of European Sports Practice was Philippe Blatter, nephew of the FIFA president. According to FIFA spokesman Andreas Herren, Philippe 'supported the McKinsey team as an expert . . . however he is not in charge of the work at FIFA'.

FIFA people who don't have a photo of Philippe in the family album could look him up on McKinsey's website. He's handsome, athletic and beside his picture is one of those McKinsey mission-blurbs they seem to like so much. Philippe asks, 'What is the point of getting up in the morning if you can't believe that something extraordinary will happen to you?'

Philippe did triathlons, played tennis and spent a vacation driving through the deserts of Yemen. He'd recently worked in Argentina and Brazil and now he'd head a team that worked on 'a client service mission' to encourage Uncle's managers to new heights of efficiency. Philippe didn't spend a lot of time on site but his youthful five-strong team were given offices in the 'chicken house', a building that had once housed a miniature zoo belonging to the city of Zurich. According to McKinsey, these were 'team-rooms often used at the client's site to optimise work efficiency'. Disgruntled FIFA staffers immediately labelled them 'the green-horns'.

First they looked at jazzing up Blatter's US$100 million scheme to build offices and training pitches for the poorer national associations. This was called the Goal Bureau project, and it was chaired by Qatar's Mohamed Bin Hammam. The greenhorns got to work, deploying the language of management-speak that was soon echoing around the corridors of Sunny Hill and in the bars after work as staff tried to puzzle out what was going on.

It was all rather comical. FIFA was rent with bitterness, conspiracies and back-stabbing, there was a seismic power struggle between the President and his chief executive, and the greenhorns, oblivious in the chicken house to the grinding of football's tectonic plates beneath their feet, enthused about 'aspiration-setting workshops'.

At the end of every month Dr Jens Abend, boss of McKinsey's Zurich office, sent in his bill. Come Christmas 2000, Abend popped in one for a couple of months' consulting fees, plus 20 per cent in expenses, and the bottom line said 903,000 francs (almost £400,000). That was a lot of money, even by FIFA's standards. It was way above the maximum grant to any of the poorer countries FIFA was supposed to be helping.

Month after month jargon rolled out of the chicken house and Dr Abend's big bills rolled in. To pay McKinsey's mounting fees FIFA had to tighten some belts. Not Sepp's, though. Staffers had their working away from home allowance slashed by half to US$100 a day. Then the greenhorns knocked 5 million francs off the refereeing budget and cut FIFA's donations to charity by 550,000 francs.

FIFA workers, who'd had their tools updated, their aspirations reset and their allowances slashed, puzzled over the greenhorns' strenuous efforts and dubious results. They may perhaps have thought that McKinsey were being used unknowingly to undermine Zen-Ruffinen, by showing him how 'innovative' he should have been. If all the gobbledygook had any meaning it seemed to be saying, 'You haven't been running this place the right way, Michel. You're inefficient, incapable, out of touch with modern management techniques. We are the cutting edge of business science, we are the massed ranks of the McKinsey MBAs. We know best!'

One frosty night McKinsey's greenhorns swept FIFA's workers out of Sunny Hill and off to the curling rink at Ruti. The greenhorns split them into two teams and told them to slip into special shoes, then had them hurling lumps of granite across the ice and danced in their path with sweeping brushes. Greenhorns made careful notes on everybody's performance. Zen-Ruffinen was dragged along and people noticed that he seemed to feel the night's chill.

No sooner had their curling aches and pains faded than the poor FIFA people were off again to a country hotel 20 km from Zurich. They were split into two groups, led to identical rooms and given two minutes to look at a pile of wooden beams and planks – something like Lego for grownups. Then they were pulled out.

'You have seen the materials,' a greenhorn told the baffled football administrators. 'Now you will appoint a project leader from your ranks. You have 15 minutes to design a bridge from what we have shown you. Then you must build it.' The team led by Zen-Ruffinen did well and the other didn't, the greenhorns took more notes and Dr Abend sent another bill for the good of the game. Blatter later praised their work, saying it was of the highest quality and of tremendous benefit to FIFA. McKinsey don't come cheap, and in total, FIFA paid them at least £2 million.

MCKINSEY BOAST that they're not scared to confront clients with unpalatable truths. If the boss is leading a business in the wrong direction, McKinsey will tell him. They claim they've even told bosses to quit, for the good of their company.

I asked McKinsey's London office, was Philippe working for

Sepp or for FIFA? Did Philippe get any bonuses for bringing in £2 million worth of fees? McKinsey's spokesman, Tony Danker, gushed, 'I am glad we could work together on this!' Then he told me the work was confidential and he was unable to comment.

15

A MESSIAH FOR TRINIDAD

The rise and rise of Jack Warner

'JACK WARNER is a wonderful and loyal friend. He is very competent and I just have to say that Jack is one of the top personalities in the world of football.'

Ask around the twin islands of Trinidad and Tobago and few people share Sepp's opinion of Jack. Many say he's a dictator who's built his power climbing up on other people's backs, a man who's become richer as he's climbed up the FIFA ladder.

But why the hostility? Why should people feel so passionate about Sepp's loyal friend, a man who has taken tea with the Queen at Buckingham Palace – and chided her that British companies were failing to spend their sponsorship money on football in Trinidad & Tobago?

We've met Jack already, levering an attractive babe into Haitian Dr Kyss's seat to vote in more power for Jack in Zurich in 1996. And we met him again, levering his friend Neville Ferguson into poor old Dr Kyss's seat to vote for Sepp Blatter in 1998.

Warner's a mover, a shaker, a fixer, a manipulator, he's the man whose entrepreneurialism and cheek tells us so much about Blatter's FIFA. And he's the man who, unchecked, could find himself FIFA president within the decade.

At home in Trinidad & Tobago he says he owns shopping malls, hotels, offices and warehouses. He claims to have 'a few businesses' in the United States, purchased, he told a reporter, 'with the salary and allowances I received from FIFA. I have had one or two good fortunes'. He says that as a FIFA vice-president, he receives 'ultra-fantastic paycheques'. Estimates of his wealth range between £10 million and £20 million.

When not the centre of attention Warner looks a bit sulky. He tends to slump in his chair, slide his short legs forward, throw his head back. He's an image of brightly flowered ties, crisp white shirts, blue suits and glossily polished shoes. Jack looks studious in his large-framed gold-rimmed glasses. On one wrist he wears a chunky gold bangle, on the other a chunky gold watch. He wears, one, two, three fat gold rings. At play, Jack wears a brightly patterned shirt, open at the neck to display a thick gold chain.

He's been a favourite of Trinidad's corruption-prone UNC party led by Baseo Panday. In government they gave him a special diplomatic passport. Flexing his muscles at FIFA underlings back in 2001 he made this astonishing assertion: 'I am a senior member in the Gov't of T&T and, effective from this Thursday 15 August, Chairman of the Airports Authority.' Neither claim was true, though he certainly gave Panday's discredited regime a lot of support and a lot of money, much of it from football.

When Panday's government fell Warner went on the stump for the UNC, describing political opponents as 'Taliban'. He told voters in the constituency of La Brea that on a recent trip to New York he had obtained TT$2.5 million from FIFA to build a sports centre in La Brea. There was one condition. They had to vote in UNC man Norris Ferguson. 'If he don't win, no sports, simple as that,' said Warner.

A hung parliament followed and Panday's crew rewarded Warner by nominating him as Speaker, although he wasn't an MP. The nomination failed. Even some of Panday's supporters shunned him.

OUR JACK Warner story starts in January 1943. Warner was born, in his own words, 'a poor black boy' in Rio Claro in the south of the island of Trinidad, a church-loving child with a passion for the movies, an unpopular boy who knew unhappy times at school. Fellow pupils treated him as an outsider and dirtied his school uniform.

Jack and some other lanky youths queued up outside St James's Barracks in 1961 to sign up as police cadets. What a different life he might have led. A life of contentment shaking down speeding motorists for a handful of crinkly notes and setting about the citizenry with his night stick after closing time.

It wasn't to be. Jack's mum and his parish priest pounded up, grabbed Jack by the collar and marched him home. No, Jack was going to be a teacher. And that was that.

Jack trained as a teacher (though when his mum wasn't looking he signed up for the Special Reserve Police, known to the island's wags as Something Resembling Police). He soon learned that power was something he enjoyed. He agitated briefly in Trinidad's Black Power movement, and then spotted a bigger opportunity: football.

The first black man to run football in Trinidad was Eric James who took the secretary's seat in 1942. For nearly three decades James earned a reputation as a decent man, a man of principle who, like his brother CLR James, the celebrated cricket writer and political thinker, served his people and sport unselfishly as Trinidad found its post-colonial feet.

Getting rich out of sport was furthest from their minds. Within months of Eric James's retirement Warner had taken over the association and was running it in a whole new way. He created new organisations that seemed to have no clear purpose and could exercise voting rights should his position come under threat. According to Jack, he and his friends were lending large sums of money to the association but, with endearing modesty, not all of them wished to be named.

The press attacked him. He's running a dictatorship, they said. Jack himself joked that he had 'one set of books for the clubs, one for the public and one for the Sports Minister'.

Jack is, by his own account, close to God. In the biography he commissioned for himself in 1998 from Tino Singh, sports editor of the Trinidad *Guardian*, Jack's sister recalls his brilliance as a child, always able to defeat her at checkers. He loved Sundays because 'there was always something to learn from the sermons'. And he learned, 'never to try and fool God'.

'My husband would never have achieved any of the things he did if he was dishonest . . . he is close to his Creator,' says his wife Maureen, whose credit card is said to have one of the highest limits in Trinidad.

Jack had planned to call his biography *A Prophet Without Honour* to suggest his messianic qualities in a country where he endures widespread loathing. But he stumbled across a better title, *Upwards Through the Night*, from the poet Henry Longfellow: '*The heights by great men reached and kept were not attained by sudden flight, but they, while their companions slept, were toiling upward in the night.*'

It's true, there was a little sleepiness, a lack of vigilance, around Trinidad where people had become accustomed to sports administrators from the James brothers mould.

One of Eric James's achievements was setting up the Caribbean Football Union but it was Warner who saw that the Union offered a stepping stone to greater power. In 1983 he ran successfully for the presidency and that gave him an automatic seat on FIFA's executive committee. Biographer Tino Singh, recorded this was 'a step that created major revenue earning opportunities'.

President Havelange, nine years in power, recognised Warner's qualities, and promoted him. For the next six years Warner learned to say what the Gulf billionaires wanted to hear, attended the Olympics as an honoured guest and lived the lifestyle he had dreamed.

FEW THINGS unite a little country like success in world sport. The streets of Trinidad & Tobago were alive with happiness. Calypsos blared from bars and sound trucks. People walked tall and smiled. Trinidad was one game away from qualifying for the 1990 World Cup. Little Trinidad! They were On the Road to Rome. All they had to do was draw with the Americans at the national stadium on 19 November 1989 and they'd be off to Italy.

Coach Gally Cummings, one of Trinidad's most respected former players, who'd turned out for the New York Cosmos, took his team away from the ceaseless drumming, the interfaith services of hope and the overflowing rum shops and mentored them quietly at their camp at Fyzabad in Trinidad's oil belt, 50 miles from Port of Spain.

These were fantastic days for the squad. Their whole nation was behind them. And, they felt, the whole world. Who could resist the happy notion of this little island defeating the super-power?

As the Trinidad team trained, Jack Warner, secretary still of the association, made preparations of his own. He printed thousands of extra tickets for the match and drove a coach and horses through the rules forbidding alcohol sales at the stadium.

Jack seemed to have gone from having God close by, to being God himself: *Let the multitudes come! Let the fans drink! Turn orange squash into beer! Let the profits roll in!*

Come the day excitement in Trinidad was explosive. It seemed the entire country was going to the game. It seemed like that thanks to Jack's decision to print all those extra tickets. Tens of thousands of fans swathed in red and waving their precious tickets surrounded the stadium, far more than it could possibly accommodate. Match stewards, fearful for fans' safety, opened the gates early. Soon every aisle was blocked with fans standing. The stadium bulged. The bar opened. People started drinking. Meanwhile, outside, thousands of people who'd spent their hard-earned cash on Trinidad's biggest match in living memory found they couldn't get near the stadium. And they were angry.

As Jack Warner enjoyed pre-match drinks in the VIP lounge with Horace Burrell from Jamaica and Colin Klass from Guyana, fans chanted curses against him. Through the melée glided the air-conditioned luxury coach bearing the US squad. Trinidad's little minibus couldn't get through the angry crowd. Eventually Trinidad's finest footballers were manhandled over the heads of the crowd and into the stadium.

It wasn't, perhaps, the best preparation for the game. The Americans scored a single goal and were off to Italy. Trinidad was devastated.

According to Warner's biography, Havelange and Blatter were downcast. They'd been silently backing the underdogs, said Warner, and felt so bad that they gave Trinidad a fair play award in an effort to console them. As for Warner himself, he was so upset, he claimed, that tears streamed down his face. He felt suicidal. He threw himself down on his secretary's couch and sobbed his heart out.

The local press meanwhile accused Warner of 'massive fraud'. According to the Trinidad *Guardian*, 45,000 tickets had been printed for the game, even though the stadium would hold only 28,500 fans. It went on to say, '35,000 patrons jammed into the stadium before midday when the gates were closed . . . Such was the overcrowding that several persons fainted from the heat and had to be treated. Fire officials said that the situation was high risk.'

Warner stonewalled. The media wouldn't let up and after four days he finally decided to call a press conference. National association president Peter O'Connor sat to one side, arms folded on the tabletop, looking as if his proximity to Warner was giving him piles. General Secretary Warner was the passionate one, both hands pressed flat to his bosom as he leaned forward and begged the hacks to believe him.

Warner initially told FIFA that he had sold 43,000 tickets in total – 10,000 to corporate Trinidad & Tobago to enable the association to pay off its debt (although he had not told colleagues about his plan), 28,000 on the open market, and 5,000 reserved for 'emergency use'. Now at this press briefing he claimed that the association had printed and sold only 28,500 tickets and argued that the stadium's figure of 34,834 tickets was wrong. *At least 6,000 of the tickets were bogus!*

The government appointed a retired QC to lead a commission of inquiry into the scandal. Lionel Seemungal, reading through some papers about the breaches of safety rules, pondered aloud: 'Did Warner believe he was God or merely think he was running the country?' Warner leapt on the comment, and went to court to have Seemungal removed. He failed but the inquiry eventually ground to a halt, leaving Warner claiming he wasn't able to tell his side of the story.

He did his best in his approved biography with it's glowing introduction from Havelange – he offers it for sale at US$20 a time from his office in Port of Spain. Printing the extra tickets and then initially denying it had to be confronted. Biographer Tino Singh explained, 'Warner's later credibility would be undermined by this single action. What had in fact been a series of critical errors of judgement – to sell more tickets than the stadium could properly accommodate, to hold even more tickets to meet a "special" demand, and, worst of all, to keep his executive completely out of the picture – was now complicated by a fabrication, a denial and an attempt to create a smokescreen around what had really transpired. By compounding his initial error, Warner now made any later explantion or clarification further fodder for the gristmill of innuendo, rumour and overt hostility.'

Singh went on to say: 'The public perception was that Warner had personally pocketed the proceeds from the sale of the extra tickets. This was of course not true – the audit performed on the accounts of the game afterwards by Ernst & Young revealed that all the tickets had been properly accounted for, including the 5,000 "extra" tickets Warner had reserved. But by the time that audit became public, no one seemed to care. Warner's name had already been irreversibly besmirched.'

Surely a prophet was never so unwelcome in his own country as Jack Warner. His disillusionment culminated in his resignation as Secretary of the association shortly afterwards. But there was good news. The day after the match, according to Jack's biography, he heard a knock on his door. In walked the immensely round, shirt-button popping figure of Charles Gordon Blazer, forever known as Chuck, a vice-president of the US soccer federation, Commissioner of the American Soccer League, and believed to have a 24/7 full service McDonald's built into his bedroom closet. They'd got to know each other on the CONCACAF circuit and Chuck brought glad tidings.

'Jack, you have done enough for your country,' proclaimed the American. 'But they have never accepted you. CONCACAF is in the doldrums. Use your skills to help build it up.'

Football was never to be the same again. On the horizon was the next CONCACAF election. If Chuck and Jack could prise the presidency from the longtime grasp of Mexico's ageing Joaquin Soria Terrazas and turn the region's 35 votes into a solid voting block at FIFA, they would be among the most powerful men in the world game.

Whoever replaced Terrazas would need the virtues of 'a Gandhi or a Martin Luther King', reflected Blazer. Warner, he was sure, had these qualities in abundance. Jack the Messiah had found his John the Baptist.

CHAPTER NOTES

Chapter 1

page 1. The story of the bribe that was wrongly addressed: Multiple sources inside and outside FIFA and ISL. Parts published in the *Daily Mail*, 27 May 2002 and again on 5 December 2005. Also published in various Swiss and German newspapers. More in Chapter 7.

page 4. Repression in Tunisia is widely recorded by varied organisations from the *New York Times* to the BBC and NGOs such as *Reporters Sans Frontiers* and Amnesty.

page 5. The decision of the Zurich prosecutor and his investigation of allegations against Sepp Blatter are dealt with fully in Chapter 29.

page 6. The author's question to Blatter was taped by a film crew from Denmark and subsequently broadcast in many European countries. The film's producer and interviewer was German journalist Jens Weinreich.

Chapter 2

I am grateful to Morley Myers and Keith Botsford who reported from the Frankfurt Congress and to Christian Jannette who shared his memories of working for Dassler.

I have published more on Dassler's team and its operations in three previous books *The Lords of the Rings* (1992), *The New Lords of the Rings* (1996) and *The Great Olympic Swindle* (2000) and in numerous television films and articles.

Chapter 3

page 22. Chowdhry's involvement in international amateur boxing is chronicled in my previous Olympic books and most recently, *The Great Olympic Swindle*.

page 24. André Guelfi tells his story in his autobiography *L'Original* published by Robert Laffont, Paris 1999. There's more in contemporary French press reports of the Elf-Acquitaine scandal and subsequent trial.

page 26. Dirty tricks against Kaser: Kistner & Wienreich, *Das Milliarden Spiel: Fusball, Geld und Medien* (Fischer Taschenbuch Verlag, 1998).

page 28. André Guelfi's comments about Blatter's hiring by FIFA and Kaser's pay-off following his falling out with Dassler, were recorded by Barbara Smit for her story of the Adidas-Puma family story, published in the UK in May 2006 by Penguin as *Pitch Invasion* and in several translations.

Chapter 4

Thanks to Ezequiel Fernandez Moores for his guidance on all matters Argentine. His work on FIFA senior vice-president and Finance Committee chairman Julio Grondona has been a blessing for foreign reporters.

page 35. Blatter's attempt to succeed Havelange was reported in detail by Kistner and Weinreich in *Das Milliarden Spiel: Fusball, Geld und Medien*, and in contemporaneous reports.

The issue came up again in 1998 when Blatter ran for FIFA president. See 'Soccer-Johansson launches blistering attack on Blatter,' *Reuters*, 27 March 1998.

page 35. Pelé accusing Havelange's son-in-law Ricardo Teixeira of corruption: *International Herald Tribune*, 15 December 1993.

page 36. Investigation of Havelange in *Playboy* Brazil, 1994 by Roberto José Pereira.

page 36. Ellert Schramm, quoted in Kistner & Weinreich, *Das Milliarden Spiel: Fusball, Geld und Medien*.

page 37. Havelange and 32 teams in the WC Finals – quoted in Kistner & Weinreich, *Das Milliarden Spiel: Fusball, Geld und Medien*.

Chapter 5

Birth of the FIFA gambling plan: I am grateful to Rodrigo Mattos and Juca Kfouri in Brazil for their assistance with this investigation.

Much of the detail of the gambling plan is revealed in a memo from Richard Herson to Blatter, 28 May 2001.

page 45. The detail of the Machline helicopter crash is recorded at the National Transportation Safety Board http://www.ntsb.gov/ntsb /brief.asp?ev_id=20001206X01950&key=1

page 46. The 1,600-page report by Brazil's Congress on football corruption was published on 4 December 2001. It gives fascinating detail on the other financial relationships of the main players in the FIFA gambling plan.

Chapter 6

The shock of the ISL directors on losing the Olympic contract and the need to retain, at all costs, the FIFA contract is reflected in the ISL board minutes of 7 December 1995.

Chapter 7

page 60. The wrongly addressed payment. The anonymous quote from a former FIFA official was checked with him before publication.

Chapter 8

page 61. Havelange 'honoured' to be a guest of President Abacha, in 'Havelange apologizes to Nigeria', *Reuters*, 8 November 1995.

page 63. *Sunday Times* article 'Havelange defends Nigerian plans despite condemnation,' by Peter Wilson quoted by *Reuters*, 12 November 1995.

page 64. David Will rejects gifts, quoted in *Badfellas*, by John Sugden and Allan Tomlinson (Mainstream, 2003).

page 66. Dr Jean-Marie Kyss was interviewed by the author in his surgery and also in the national stadium in Port au Prince in April 2002.

page 67. Vincy Jalal named as the delegate from the Haiti national association on page 6 of the Minutes of FIFA's 50th Congress, Zurich, 3/4 July 1996.

page 70. Johansson; 'I will push for an independent accountant,' *AP*, 21 March 1998.

page 71. For more details of Chet Greene's ticket order – see Chapter 28.

page 72. The UEFA-sponsored resolution to force Blatter to declare his candidacy was dated 12 March 1998. The meeting was reported by *Reuters*, *AP* and *AFP* on 12 and 13 March.

Chapter 9

page 75. Platini: 'I'm a man of conviction,' *Reuters*, 18 May 1998.

page 75. Blatter will be transparent: 'Blatter Says He's Near FIFA Victory,' *AP*, 5 June 1998.

page 75. Johansson expects a dirty campaign: 'Blatter is Havelange's puppet, says Johansson,' *Reuters*, 29 March 1998.

page 77. Braun's comments were at UEFA's congress in April 1998, open to the media.

page 78. Johansson in Kuala Lumpur: 'Havelange is not neutral,' *Reuters*, 14 May 1998.

page 79. Blatter's brief visit to Nairobi was extensively reported at the time in the *Daily Nation* and *East African Standard*.

page 81. Blatter's US$135,000 election budget, reported by *Reuters* on 5 June 1998 and then US$300,000 by *AP* later the same day.

page 81. Platini objecting to 5-star hotels: 'FIFA presidential hopeful says he's near victory,' *AP*, 5 June 1998.

page 82. Farah Addo was interviewed in Bamako, Mali, in January 2002 by the author with Christoph Mueller of Swiss TV, SFDRS.

page 85. Emir's plane: Blatter interviewed in *Tages Anzeiger*, 23 December 1998.

Chapter 10

page 89. 'Bomba' Mthethwa in the *Swaziland Times*, 5 June 1998.

page 90. Neville Ferguson of Trinidad passing himself off as the delegate from Haiti is recorded on Page 9 of the minutes of the 1998 FIFA Congress. The episode was recorded on the official FIFA video.

page 92. Corinne Blatter on African support, *Reuters*, 8 June 1998.

page 92. Warner's 'pivotal role', *Trinidad Express*, 12 July 1998.

page 92. Rumours of US$50,000 bundles being handed out to African delegates were reported in the *Washington Post*, 9 June 1998 and elsewhere.

page 92. Blatter 'vehemently' denying: 'Blatter threatens to sue over rumours,' *Reuters*, 9 June 1998.

page 92. Graham Kelly and Alec McGivan: 'England relieved with Blatter victory', *Reuters*, 8 June 1998.

CHAPTER NOTES

Chapter 11

page 96. Blatter charging his election expenses to FIFA (and subsequently repaying this sum) is evidenced in his claim form and other documents seen by the author.

page 99. The author has seen a notarised statement sworn by a former FIFA official stating the facts of Blatter's bonus. See also Cartier letter to author on page 306.

page 103. Markus Siegler revealing that FIFA Executive Committee members do not have to produce receipts when they submit expenses; email to *Daily Mail*, 2 September 2003.

Chapter 12

page 105. Urs Linsi's declaration that FIFA is transparent, posted in January 2003, appears to have been erased from fifa.com. It was at: http://www.fifa.com/Service/MR_A/51043_E.html

page 106. Chung letter to Warner regarding Blatter's salary, 18 January 2002.

page 107. Warner's reply to Chung letter, 21 January 2002.

page 108. Blatter's Appenzell tax affairs featured in *Blick* in September 1995. The story was picked up by most of the Swiss media in the following months.

Chapter 13

page 115. Johansson 'I have no proof of this and I refuse to speculate' in 'Blatter threatens to sue over rumours,' *Reuters*, 9 June 1998.

page 115. The membership of FIFA committees can be found at: http://www.fifa.com/en/organisation/committee.execom.html.

page 116. Warner's wealth: *Trinidad Guardian*, 13 January 2000.

page 118. Koloskov's $100,000. See Michel Zen-Ruffinen report of 3 May 2002 and Blatter's subsequent 'Rectification' document.

Chapter 14

page 122. Thanks to several French reporters who helped me with background on Jerome Champagne.

Chapter 15

Sources include: a) Warner's authorised biography *Upwards Through the Night*, written by Tino Singh, sports editor of the *Trinidad Guardian* and published in 1998 by Lexicon of Trinidad Ltd; and b) 'The Story of Trinidad and Tobago Football 1983–2000' compiled by Valentino Singh (Chapter 12 – 'Austin Jack Walker' and Chapter 15 – 'Aftershocks') – T&TFF website: www.tnt.fifa.com.

page 131. Blatter praises his 'wonderful and loyal friend' Warner, 25 September 2001.

page 132. Diplomatic Passport – from Prime Minister Panday on Warner's 57th birthday, 26 January 2000.

page 132. Warner says his opponents are 'Taliban', *Trinidad Express* 26 November 2001.

page 132. Warner promises sports facility to La Brea constituency, *Trinidad Express* 26 November 2001.

page 133. Warner nominated as Speaker of Trinidad parliament; *Trinidad Guardian*, 10 April 2001.

page 134. Warner's three sets of books. *Upwards Through the Night*, page 136.

page 137. Warner printed thousands of extra tickets, Trinidad v USA World Cup Qualifier 1990, *Upwards Through the Night*, pages 25–47 and 'The Story of Trinidad and Tobago Football 1983–2000,' Chapter 15.

ACKNOWLEDGEMENTS

You can't chase the bad guys without help from the good guys, and it's the good ones who make my work a joy. Thanks to all of you.

Some brave and principled people have taken personal risks to shine a light into the secret world of international football. For obvious reasons I won't name them here. They have my respect and warmest thanks.

Here are the ones I can name.

Colin Gibson, as sports editor of the *Daily Mail*, commissioned me to travel the world investigating FIFA and had the courage to run stories that scared the pants off other editors.

Thomas Kistner of the Munich *Süddeutsche Zeitung* and Jens Weinreich of the *Berliner Zeitung* shared intelligence, friendship and laughter. I recommend their 1998 book *Das Milliarden Spiel: Fusball, Geld und Medien*. Jean François Tanda at Zurich's *Sonntags Zeitung* broke a string of stories at FIFA in 2005 that were followed world-wide.

Veteran journalist Keith Botsford offered his stories, wisdom and wit on the era of Joao Havelange. Morley Myers, still on the beat, still at every major sports event, recalled Frankfurt in 1974 with gusto.

Barbara Smit shared her painstaking research on the Dassler

family. Her *Pitch Invasion* will be essential reading for anyone who wants to learn more about how corporations took over world sport, trained its officials to be obedient and found intriguing ways to bribe them.

Rafael Marques in Angola told me how he was jailed on the demand of Justino José Fernandes, a member of FIFA's internal audit committee. In Kenya, I was guided by newspaperman Elias Makori, Bob Munro of the Mathere project that uses football to help kids from the slums, and agent Simon Wiseman. In Uganda Stephen Ouma Bwire briefed me on who was stealing the national association's money. In Nigeria, Olukayode Thomas told me where to go looking for evidence.

Bob Wagman gave me an education in American soccer and in Argentina Ezequiel Fernandes Moores shared his knowledge of Julio Grondona and the Generals' World Cup of 1978. Rodrigo Mattos in Brazil taught me about Joao Havelange and Ricardo Teixeira and their FIFA gambling business, and generously handed over his cache of letters and contracts.

Fans and administrators in Trinidad told me illuminating stories about life with Jack Warner. Emile Elias of the Contractors' Association and Selby Browne of Caribbean Sports Television Network were especially helpful. Raffique Shah and George Hislop recalled Jack's early days. Journalist Lasana Liburd gave excellent guidance, even as he broke new ground.

In Mexico City and Miami Edgardo Codesal briefed me on his experiences with Warner and Blazer.

Dr Jean-Marie Kyss spared his precious time in Port au Prince to talk modestly about his battles to preserve football's assets from government gangsters. Kalai and Ron Bluntschli interpreted, drove and educated me about Haiti.

Ian 'Magic' Hughes drew me to Antigua with his groundbreaking reporting of the extraordinary abuse of FIFA grants.

Alex Tomlinson shared with me his (unsuccessful) attempts to persuade the IOC's president Jacques Rogge to let the island's youngsters participate in the qualifying rounds of the Athens Olympic tournament. Gordon Derrick helped me make sense of the mess of papers that were the national association's accounts and Noel Egan introduced me to the young people at the grass-roots who'd never seen a penny of FIFA's money.

Jens Sejer Andersen in Denmark brings together so many digging reporters at 'Play the Game' conferences; connections made there have produced lots of great stories – for me and reporters all over the world. In Barcelona Xavier Vinyals i Capdepon never gave up in the quest for a picture of Juan Antonio Samaranch doing something he'd prefer you didn't know about. After 15 years, Xavier found it.

Christian Jannette quarried his memories of the Dassler years and Eric Wattez helped me research in France and guided the French translators of this book. Laurent Coadic at *L'Équipe* explained the relationship between France and FIFA. In Tunis, David Barnes, now freelancing in Provence, told me some of the funniest stories of the Dassler legacy.

Switzerland's Christoph Mueller was a great colleague in Mali. We worked and laughed in Bamako and again back in Zurich. Christoph introduced me to his colleague Urs Schnell from the weekly *Rundschau* programme who spent many hours explaining the details of the ISL liquidation. Zora Ledergerber of Swiss Transparency International gave me an insight into Markus Siegler's heavy-handed tactics.

Zurich investigating magistrate Urs Hubmann was generous with his wisdom and time as was ISL liquidator Thomas Bauer – despite a raging toothache.

Osama El-Sheikh, managing editor of *Super* magazine helped in Tunis. Back in England Neil Wilson of the *Daily Mail* generously shared his knowledge of ISL's history. At the *Mail* Matt Lawton and Martin Lipton, Paul Newman, Charles Sale, John Greechan, Victoria Jackson and the Sports Desk crew gave solid support.

David Bond at the *Evening Standard*, Gordon Farquhar at *BBC Sport* and Brian Oliver at the *Observer* opened my eyes to other aspects of Blatter's FIFA. David Pallister at the *Guardian* remembered Morocco's hasty exit from the Organisation of African Unity to continue plundering the Western Sahara and Toby Shelley of the *Financial Times* shared his deep understanding of the region and its politics.

As always Michael Gillard gave masterly advice. Peter Jackson and others gave me the assistance – and sometimes interventions – of seasoned detectives. Denis O'Connor looked at KPMG's way of presenting FIFA's financial information. Accountant Richard Woods advised me how to interpret KPMG's private advice to Blatter on the curiosities they found when they took over FIFA's audit.

Caroline Wood brought order to my research. Christopher Whiteley enthusiastically led me through heaps of German language documents and Azucena Fernandez Durán explained the Spanish ones. Mathew D. Rose steered me through the intricacies of legal High German. When the Great Cumbrian storm of January 2005 severed my power lines in the hills, Tom and Andri Thwaites gave me shelter and electricity.

Warm thanks are due to my agent Sheila Crowley and my editor Tom Whiting at HarperSport, and to Clare Sambrook for bringing her wit and energy to the editing.